Family Counseling: A Guide for Professionals

Family Counseling: A Guide for Professionals

Abigail Hardy

STATES
ACADEMIC PRESS
www.statesacademicpress.com

Family Counseling: A Guide for Professionals
Abigail Hardy
ISBN: 978-1-63989-810-7 (Hardback)

Published by States Academic Press,
109 South 5th Street,
Brooklyn, NY 11249, USA

Visit us on the World Wide Web at:
www.statesacademicpress.com

Cataloging-in-Publication Data

Family counseling : a guide for professionals / Abigail Hardy.
p. cm.
Includes bibliographical references and index.
ISBN 978-1-63989-810-7
1. Family counseling--Vocational guidance. 2. Family counselors--Vocational guidance. I. Hardy, Abigail.
HV697 .F36 2023
362.828 6--dc23

Table of Contents

Preface

Family relationships are important for psychological health. Family counseling is a branch of psychotherapy. Family counselors work with families and couples to nurture change and development. When problems develop within families or among couples, counseling can help them to resolve marital problems, overcome challenges, and resolve issues such as anxiety, depression, etc. Adoption counseling ensures positive outcomes with adopted children and teens, and their proper integration in the family. A family therapist should be able to influence conversations such that mutual strengths and support are enhanced. A wide range of counseling techniques are used such as structural and strategic therapy, narrative therapy, transgenerational therapy, communication theory, reality therapy, genogram, etc. Therapy interventions focus on relationship patterns instead of analyzing childhood traumas or the impulses of the unconscious mind. This book elucidates the principles and techniques of family counseling in a holistic manner. While understanding the long-term perspectives of the topics, the book makes an effort in highlighting their impact as a modern tool for the development of stronger familial relationships and resolution of disputes. It is a complete source of knowledge on the present status of this important field.

To facilitate a deeper understanding of the contents of this book a short introduction of every chapter is written below:

Chapter 1- Family counseling is a branch of psychotherapy aimed at couples and families in intimate relationships. It seeks to promote change and development for better psychological health through direct participation of each concerned member in the therapy sessions. The aim of this chapter is explore the importance and goals of family counseling, ethics in family counseling, grief counseling and crisis intervention counseling as well as guide clients for healing from childhood trauma, dealing with a bipolar family member, etc.

Chapter 2- Family therapy requires a range of counseling methods and techniques such as structural therapy, narrative therapy, transgenerational therapy, strategic therapy, relationship counseling and education, etc. This chapter explores the techniques and exercises of family counseling for guiding clients in building better relationship, using art and play-based activities, creating a genogram, using genograms for psychotherapy, etc.

Chapter 3- Depending on the conflict at hand, therapy may be targeted at analyzing previous instances of conflict or the sources of conflict through a better understanding of patterns of interaction. Therapists may also focus on the management and solution of problems rather than in the identification of a single cause. This chapter has been carefully written to provide an overview of family constellation therapy, strategic and structural family therapy, transgenerational family therapy, narrative therapy, etc.

Chapter 4- Marriage counseling or marriage therapy is aimed at improving romantic relationships and resolving interpersonal conflicts. The topics elucidated in this chapter address some of the techniques of couples counseling for conflict resolution, premarital counseling, divorce therapy, family planning counseling, etc.

Chapter 5- Families need support before and after adoption in the form of pre-adoption and post-adoption counseling. Such therapy sessions allow parents to understand the emotional and behavioral needs of an adopted child. Behavior counseling is focused at changing behaviors of a concerned individual through therapy. Dealing with anger management issues, suicidal tendencies, depression, etc. are within the scope of this field. This chapter explores some of the fundamental aspects of child adoption and behavioral counseling and includes the ways to tackle simple and complex issues faced by clients in these domains.

Finally, I would like to thank the entire team involved in the inception of this book for their valuable time and contribution. This book would not have been possible without their efforts. I would also like to thank my friends and family for their constant support.

Abigail Hardy

Understanding Family Counseling

1

Family counseling is a branch of psychotherapy aimed at couples and families in intimate relationships. It seeks to promote change and development for better psychological health through direct participation of each concerned member in the therapy sessions. The aim of this chapter is explore the importance and goals of family counseling, ethics in family counseling, grief counseling and crisis intervention counseling as well as guide clients for healing from childhood trauma, dealing with a bipolar family member, etc.

Family Counseling

Family counseling is also known as family therapy. Family therapy is a branch of psychotherapy that is meant to help initiate change and nurture development in intimate relationships between family members and couples.

The job of the family therapist is to facilitate conversations that act as catalysts to strengthen and improve existing connections between family members and/or loved ones.

The average number of family therapy sessions is 5-20 but the number of sessions truly depends on the situation the family or group is involved with. The important piece of family therapy is not in the number of people involved in the session but the analytical framework and perspective. Family and couples therapy is considered to be a very effective method of treatment for several mental health concerns. There are a great number of family therapies to learn about and we start with just a few below. The descriptions of these therapies are in no way definitive or exhaustive, and are meant to provide an general idea of what they are and what may make them different.

There are a range of counseling techniques used for family therapy including:

Structural Therapy

Structural family therapy is a theory developed by Salvador Minuchin. The focus of the therapy is based on five specific principles. The five specific principles include:

- The structural therapist focuses on the interactions between people rather than their individual psyches.
- "Matrix of identity" based on personal interactions within the family.
- Family structure based on social interactions.
- "Wellfunctioning family" based on how family responds and develops according to family needs.
- The position of a family therapist is to help the family outgrow constraining growth patterns and develop as a stronger entity.

Strategic Therapy

Strategic therapy is a theory that has evolved from a combined number of a variety of psychotherapy practices. There are five different parts to strategic therapy including a brief social stage, the problem stage, interactional stage, the goal-setting stage and the task-setting stage.

Systemic Therapy

Systemic Therapy is rooted from family therapy or something known as family systems therapy. There are a number of family systems therapies that contribute to the current systemic therapy concept. In recent decades, systemic therapy has moved away from linear causality and now approaches problems as they are created in a social and linguistically influenced reality.

Narrative Therapy

Narrative therapy is different in that it encourages the person to be their own individual and to use their own skill set to address the problem and also to minimize the tiny problems in day-to-day life. The idea of narrative therapy is that in life, people create personal stories that help them identify who they are and also that they possess the proper tools to navigate their lives. The point of narrative therapy is to help clarify, develop and support the narrator in life and help guide their journey.

Transgenerational Therapy

Transgenerational therapy gives therapists the ability to examine interactions between individuals in a family across multiple generations. The family therapist's observations and analysis of interactions helps the therapist to grasp the core issues within the family group. In addition to current issues, the therapist may also pick up on future struggles or stressful situations. Concepts of transgenerational therapy are used frequently with other therapies to help create a lens to frame the issue being addressed in sessions.

Communication Therapy

Therapy for communication issues is a common need especially as it pertains to relationship therapy and the cited issue between the couple is lack of communication. Communication issues between individuals can start from differences in cultural backgrounds and/or personal experiences. Additional situations that may contribute to communication issues include trauma, secrecy, mental health issues, etc. There are many options for addressing communication issues whether it be for an individual's improvement or two involved in an intimate relationship. A trained therapist can help an individual decide what the best strategies may be for improving communication skills and ability. Strategies include active listening, opening lines of communication and mediated communication.

Psychoeducation

The practice of educating those with mental health conditions and their families to help empower and support them with their condition is referred to psychoeducation. Psychoeducation is a strong tool against the stigmatization of mental health conditions and those who face those challenges on a day-to-day basis. Psychoeducation is defined with four broad goals in mind:

- Transfer of information
- Medication and treatment support
- Training and support in selfhelp
- An available a safe place to vent

Relationship Counseling

Relationships are not easy and simple problems in your daily life can cause stress or add strain to any relationship. Additional problems that can contribute to the stress include chronic illness, a lack of communicating effectively, cultural differences, infidelity and mental health issues. Couples may also face issues of sexual intimacy, emotional distancing, financial difficulties and a general lack of trust. Relationship counseling begins usually when a couple is trying to decide whether to work out their problems and continue to be together or if they should move on.

A family therapist may be called upon to take on many different roles. These many roles require a family therapist to undergo a great deal of training, formal education, and testing to ensure that the therapist is up to the task.

While therapists may have different methods and preferred treatment techniques, they must all have at least a minimum level of experience with the treatment of:

- Child and adolescent behavioral problems
- Grieving
- Depression and anxiety
- LGBTQ issues
- Domestic violence
- Infertility
- Marital conflicts
- Substance abuse

In order to treat these and other family issues, therapists must:

- Observe how people interact within units
- Evaluate and resolve relationship problems
- Diagnose and treat psychological disorders within a family context
- Guide clients through transitional crises such as divorce or death
- Highlight problematic relational or behavioral patterns

- Help replace dysfunctional behaviors with healthy alternatives
- Take a holistic (mind-body) approach to wellness.

In order to gain the skills necessary to perform these functions, a family therapist usually obtains a bachelor's degree in counseling, psychology, sociology, or social work, followed by a master's degree in counseling or marriage and family therapy.

Next, the therapist will most likely need to complete two years of supervised work after graduation, for a total of 2,000 to 4,000 hours of clinical experience. When these requirements are met, the therapist will also likely need to pass a state-sanctioned exam, as well as completing annual continuing education courses.

This education and training will allow a therapist to help the clients who come to the therapist for guidance with a wide range of problems, including:

- Personal conflicts within couples or families
- Unexpected illness, death, or unemployment
- Developing or maintaining a healthy romantic relationship at any stage
- Behavioral problems in children
- Divorce or separation
- Substance abuse or addiction
- Mental health problems like depression and anxiety.

Goals of Family Therapy

In order to help a family work together towards a healthy family life, family therapists aim to aid family members in improving communication, solving family problems, understanding and handling special family situations, and creating a better functioning home environment.

More broadly, the goals of family therapy depend on the presenting problems of the clients. For example, the goals differ based on the following scenarios:

- A family member is suffering from schizophrenia or severe psychosis:

The goal is to help other family members understand the disorder and adjust to the psychological changes that the patient may be undergoing.

- Problems arising from cross-generational boundaries, such as when parents share a home with grandparents, or children are being raised by grandparents:

  In this case, the goal is to improve communication and help the family members set healthy boundaries.

- Families deviating from social norms (unmarried parents, gay couples raising children, etc.):

  The goals here are not always to address any specific internal problems, but the family members may need help coping with external factors like societal attitudes.

- Family members who come from mixed racial, cultural, or religious backgrounds:

  The goal, in this case, is to help family members further their understanding of one another and develop healthy relationships.

- One member is being scapegoated or having their treatment in individual therapy undermined:

  When one family member is struggling with feeling like the outcast or receives limited support from other family members, the goal is to facilitate increased empathy and understanding for the individual within their family and provide support for them to continue their treatment.

- The patient's problems seem inextricably tied to problems with other family members:

  In cases where the problem or problems are deeply rooted in problems with other family members, the goal is to address each of the contributing issues and solve or mitigate the effects of this pattern of problems.

- A blended family (i.e., step-family):

  Blended families can suffer from problems unique to their situations. In blended families, the goal of family therapy is to enhance understanding and facilitate healthy interactions between family members.

Family Psychotherapy: Taking it One Step Further

We tend to think of therapy and psychotherapy as two different forms of treatment, but in fact, they are the same thing. This ambiguity is enhanced when we introduce the term "counseling" as well.

In truth, therapy is simply a shortened form of the word "psychotherapy". However, counseling is sometimes called "talk therapy," blurring the lines even further.

Generally, counseling is applied in situations where an individual (or, in the case of family counseling, a family) engages the services of a counselor or other mental health professional to help with a specific problem or set of problems. Therapy, or psychotherapy, is a more in-depth and usually long-term form of treatment in which the client or clients discuss a wider range of issues and chronic patterns of problematic feelings, thoughts, and behaviors.

A family who is struggling with a situation that brings added stress, such as the death of a family member, addiction, or dire financial straits, may benefit from counseling to help them through their struggles to emerge on the other side as a stronger and more cohesive unit.

If a family is struggling with more chronic mental or behavioral problems, such as a father dealing with schizophrenia, a mother fighting depression, or a child who has been abused, psychotherapy is likely the better choice.

This type of therapy is appropriate for families with problems such as these because a family therapist has a different perspective on treatment than an individual therapist. While the individual therapist works with one client on solving or curing a problem, the family therapist views problems in the context of the "system" of the family. To solve a problem in a system, you need to consider all parts of the system.

> "Fixing the alternator in a car will not fix the problem if it also has flat tires, a faulty transmission, and a plugged exhaust pipe".

Issues within a family are similar to the car with several problems. A parent struggling with alcoholism is not a problem in isolation; the parent's struggle has likely affected their spouse and their children as well. A family therapist believes that problems must be addressed at the level of the whole family rather than on an individual level.

Benefits of Family Therapy

This more holistic approach to treating problems within a family has proven to be extremely effective in many cases. In family therapy, families can work on their problems with the guidance of a mental health professional in a safe and controlled environment.

The benefits of family therapy include:

- A better understanding of healthy boundaries and family patterns and dynamics
- Enhanced communication
- Improved problem solving
- Deeper empathy
- Reduced conflict and better anger management skills

More specifically, family therapy can improve the family relationships through:

- Bringing the family together after a crisis
- Creating honesty between family members
- Instilling trust in family members

- Developing a supportive family environment
- Reducing sources of tension and stress within the family
- Helping family members forgive each other
- Conflict resolution for family members
- Bringing back family members who have been isolated.

In addition, family therapy can enhance skills required for healthy family functioning, including communication, conflict resolution, and problem-solving. Improving these skills for each member of the family increases the potential for success in overcoming or addressing family problems. In family therapy, the focus is on providing all family members with the tools they need to facilitate healing.

How to do Family Therapy

Do Understand the Family's Identity

One of the main things that you must do when you begin family work is to look at how families identify themselves. A common mistake of most new social workers is to look at the family through the lens of services the family has or their current living situation. The best way to learn how a family identifies itself is to simply ask: "Would you say that your family is close or distant?" "Can you detail everyone you consider 'family'?" You'd be surprised by the answers you receive that can help inform treatment and give you a chance to use informal supports to help the family.

Don't Chase Chaos

When working with families, one of the many barriers that tend to arise is that they have an uncanny knack for pulling clinicians into their chaos. It can be even more difficult to avoid the chaotic atmosphere of a family when you are doing home visits. The best remedy for managing the family's chaos and your own anxiety is this: develop a concrete, succinct treatment plan that details each family member's role in treatment and each family member's goals for treatment. As families begin to succumb to life stressors, it will be easier to redirect the family back to the treatment plan and even link the family's stressors with what they are working on with you.

Do Respect the Family's Current State

As new social workers, we have a tendency to want to tell our clients what to do—not in an offensive way, but in a naïve, overtly helpful way that allows us to share our information and training. Although that's all well and good, it does not serve the family, nor does it help develop the therapeutic alliance you'll need to do deeper work. Being able to respect where each member of the family is in his or her current level of functioning and being able to speak to that level of functioning will show that you are not there to run the family's life, but rather you are there as a support for the family to heal and grow. When you are feeling tempted to give suggestions to the family on ways to improve their functioning, a good rule of thumb is to ask: "Can the family sustain this suggestion without help from me?" If the answer is no, then be patient as the family develops a new understanding of its current challenges and the solutions to them.

Don't Judge the Family's Current Skill Set

When working with families, it's often easy to see the patterns and decisions that have led the family to its current state of functioning. We are trained to see the systems that affect families and are given the tools to set the family on the right course. But hold on, grasshopper. Being able to be present with the family exactly where they are and guiding them to be a functional family is a very fine line, and it all starts with honoring the family's current set of skills. Van Hook suggests that the clinician's role in the family is to join with the family and enable its members to experience new ways to function. Through your work with the family, they will begin to practice new behaviors. But you have to do one more thing before you can just jump in and get to practicing new skills.

Do Develop a Therapeutic Alliance

Remember in the last paragraph when we talked about joining with a family so they can begin to experience a new way to function? Well, that all occurs when you are able to build a therapeutic alliance with the core family and its extended support systems. The therapeutic alliance will help create a safe space where each family member can not only practice new skills, but also process barriers to mastering those skills. This is the part that many new therapists get hung up on—being able to actively engage with a family that may be resistant to treatment. A few key ways to develop a positive alliance, or join, with the family include:

- Being on time and present during the session;
- Actively listening and asking for clarification instead of assuming;
- Being flexible with the family's schedule;
- Delivering value to the family by triaging needs (remember Maslow?); and
- Allowing the family's voice to be heard in treatment.

Don't Ignore Cultural Influences

The buzz word of our profession is cultural sensitivity, right? And, more than likely, each class in your graduate program expected you to take a cultural perspective in applying theory to practice. But as you work with families, the cultural lens has to become one of your sharpest assessment tools. Looking at everything from race, gender, and socioeconomic status to religious ideals, family rituals, and external support systems will help you get a good picture of a family's culture. I encourage new clinicians to not get hung up on what they think are going to be cultural barriers. Take inventory of your own ideas about culture and process them in supervision so you can come to families ready to hear and observe their cultural perspectives. One suggestion is to do a cultural assessment of a family that goes deeper than the intakes you perform in your agency. In this assessment, be sure to include all the aforementioned items, as well as the following aspects of a family's culture:

- Previous negative experiences in treatment;
- Coping efforts and beliefs about hope;
- Family organization (communication, leadership, roles); and
- The family's basic needs.

Do Develop a Strategic Treatment Plan

Going back to making sure that you do not get caught up in the family's maladaptive level of functioning, making sure that you have a strategic treatment plan that details the goals of treatment can be one of the keys to facilitating successful family therapy. The treatment plan should illustrate a clinical loop: assessment, diagnosis, goals, and termination. In the assessment, you'll gather all the important information about the family (history, resources, needs, and commitment to treatment). Next, you'll assign a mental health diagnosis to the identified patient (usually the person on your referral) that you establish from the assessment. Then, you'll use the assessment and diagnosis to create a goal that will help the family decrease symptoms and/or increase coping strategies. Last, you should discuss termination in this plan, so you and the family understand that treatment is not indefinite and will eventually end once goals are met. This clinical loop will help you to assess the progress of the family's treatment and allow you to pinpoint where adjustments need to be made as you traverse through treatment. Another benefit to developing a strategic treatment plan is that you can use the plan to discuss the family's symptoms and progress efficiently during your supervision.

Don't Underestimate your Countertransference

We all come from families. And if truth be told, a lot of us came into this field as a result of our experiences with our own families. Honoring this truth can help you build a therapeutic awareness, so you can begin to understand your motivations and difficulties in providing effective family therapy. When we work with families, it's not always obvious where the barriers to treatment can present themselves. As clinicians, we have a tendency to look to the families we work with to find answers to barriers in treatment. However, we can also look within ourselves to see that our own perspectives, experiences, and beliefs about families come into the way we provide services to families. It is important to discuss this countertransference with your supervisor, to rule out whether your experiences are shaping the treatment of the families you serve. And it is important to be honest with yourself about how your own family history and experiences motivate your work with families, so you do not force or undermine a family's treatment.

How to Become a Family Counselor

Here is the generic process to becoming a family counselor, but be sure to check with your state licensing board for specific requirements.

Complete a Bachelor's Degree Program and an Advanced Master's Program

The very first step to becoming a Licensed Professional Counselor specializing in families is to earn your high school diploma. Once you hold a diploma, you can enroll in a Bachelor's degree program majoring in Counseling or a related area of study like Psychology. A Bachelor's degree program will take about 4 years to complete if you have no completed credits and you are enrolled in the program full-time.

Upon completion of your undergraduate degree, you must then enroll in a Master's degree program as most states require applicants to have a minimum of a Master's to get licensed.

A Master's degree program does not include general courses, so the areas you study will be specific to counseling. You may take courses in family therapy, marriage counseling, counseling techniques, models, and research. The purpose of the Master's program is to advance your knowledge so that you are an expert in the field and not just knowledgeable. Earning your M.S. will take about 2 years if you are enrolled in classes full-time.

Fulfilling the Clinical Experience Requirements

The professional experience requirements, which must be done in a clinical setting, will vary by state. It is very important to check with your state's Board of Licensed Professional Counselors to find out how many hours of clinical supervision you need to sit for a state licensing exam. Many states require you to have between 2400 and 3000 clock hours of on-the-job experience under the supervision of a LPC. You must have face-to-face supervision for a majority of the time, and these requirements will be laid out in detail by the Board. It is important to check directly with the board for these requirements while you are still studying for a Bachelor's degree.

Taking the National Licensure Exam

All Licensed Professional Counselors are required to sit for a national licensing exam before they are eligible to practice. You will need to schedule the date in advance, pay the testing fee, submit documentation to prove that you meet the requirements to sit for the exam, and pass the test. Once you pass the test and a background check, your license will be issued and you will officially be a Family Counselor. You can also take a certification exam through the National Board for Certified Counselors if you want a specialty certification.

There will always be a need for Licensed Professional Counselors. If you would like to enter this field, the first step is enrolling in a reputable program. Be sure to choose an accredited program acknowledged by the American Psychological Association, and you'll be on your way to becoming a family counselor.

How to do Grief Counseling

Everyone experiences grief differently and there is no one way to help a person suffering from grief. Instead of trying to impose your own vision of what the grieving person needs, you should be there to offer companionship, a shoulder to cry on, and emotional validation. He will need to spend time grieving. You should tell him that his feelings are natural and encourage him to find his own way of commemorating his loved one.

Part 1. Practicing Helpful Counseling Techniques

1. Act as a companion. Each person's experience with grief is different. That means that no level of expertise will equip you to tell the person in mourning how he should respond. Your role is to provide company, listen, and validate their feelings.

- Don't tell, listen.
- Constantly reinforce that their response is normal and natural.
- Encourage them to use their own skills to cope with grief. If they are an artist, encourage them to use this ability to express his feelings.

- Help them understand and recognize their feelings.
- Help them develop a schedule that allows them to manage their daily tasks while reducing unnecessary outside stressors.
- Remember that your job is to be there, not to take away the pain. That is impossible. Your job is to support them, not to try to fix them.

2. Validate feelings. It is important to make it clear that you understand the person's feelings. Be sure that they know that such feelings are natural and that people experience grief differently. It might be useful to explain some of the common responses to grief and make it clear that they are natural.

- Those who experience instrumental grief focus on problem solving and try to control emotional responses.
- Those who experience intuitive grieving have intense emotional experiences that might include depression and thoughts about mortality.
- It is common for people to blame themselves, feel anger, hopelessness, anxiety, and withdrawal from the world.

3. Ask open questions. Don't ask leading questions or "yes" and "no" questions. Ask big, broad questions, that encourage him to think about his feelings and explore the subjects that he is interested in. Make it clear that you want to know what he feels, but are not questioning the validity of his feelings.

- Do not ask "why" questions. These make it sound as if you do not understand or support his feelings.
- Ask broad questions like "How do you feel?"

- Ask "What bothers you the most?"
- Instead of asking "Why do you feel that way?" ask "Could you give me specific examples?"

4. Paraphrase responses. When you are trying to get to the core of her problems, try giving a short summary of what you think she has told you. This will demonstrate that you are listening and might help her get a better grip on what is bothering her the most.

- If she tells you, "I stay up every night thinking about him. When I go to work I am tired and can't think clearly. I am getting more and more nervous and depressed because I can't function during the day." Ask, "So your grief is causing sleep problems that disrupt your life?"

5. Reflect his feelings. When you get a sense for how he feels, verify that you have correctly understood his emotions. This is a way to demonstrate that you are listening and that you have developed an emotional connection.

- Try, "Sounds like you are very angry about what has happened."
- Alternatively, "It sounds like you are having difficulty understanding your emotions."

6. Refrain from unsupportive behavior. Everything you do should be directed at her. Anything that

suggests your focus is elsewhere will be counterproductive. You should avoid forcing your own solutions upon her.

- Do not watch the clock.
- Do not take notes.
- Do not look around the room.
- Do not try to read too much into her feelings and impose your own idea or her feelings on her.
- Do not preach or lecture about what she should do.
- Refrain from giving too much advice or asking too many questions.
- Do not respond too quickly. Allow moments of silence.
- Do not change the subject.
- Do not talk too much about yourself.

Part 2. Developing a Supportive Persona

1. Look him in the eye. Look him in the eye to show that you are interested in and engaged with what he is saying. Allow your face to demonstrate that you are emotional and supportive. Be dynamic and engaged, possibly nodding in affirmation.

2. Keep your body open and relaxed. Crossed legs and arms may suggest that you are closed off or uninviting. Try to sit straight up, with your limbs open. Your body should appear relaxed and you can gesture with your hands to show emotional support.

- Also be sure that your body is facing directly toward the grieving person to indicate that you are engaged with her.
- Sit on the same level as the person you are talking to. Do not take a chair that allows you to tower over her, or her over you. This creates a sense of power imbalance that is not helpful for open conversation.

3. Talk like you care. Talk naturally and allow your voice to show emotion. Try to develop a soothing tone in your voice. Your conversation style should also demonstrate that you are there to listen. Don't interrupt him, jump from topic to topic, or rush him to an answer.

- It is okay to leave periods of silence. These allow him to think about his feelings and ensure that he does not feel that he has been cut off or is rushed to respond.

Part 3. Using Rituals for Remembrance

1. Get her to plan ahead for important dates. Holidays or important dates in the person's relationship with the person she lost can trigger feelings of loss. Encourage her to plan ahead to commemorate those days. This can help her create a feeling of continuity with the past or create the sense that you are moving on.

- While it is particularly useful to develop a ritual for special dates, there is no reason why the griever shouldn't plan to celebrate or remember the deceased any other day.

2. Encourage him to commemorate with ritual. There is a plethora of rituals he can use to remember his loved lost one. Which one he picks depends on his relationship with the person and what it was that once brought them together. Some examples include:

- Preparing a meal that the deceased enjoyed.
- Watch a movie that the person enjoyed.
- Go on a walk, possibly where the two of had been in the past, and remember times spent together.
- Buy flowers on important days.
- Travel somewhere the deceased wanted to go.
- Listen to music that reminds the grieving person of the deceased.
- Look through a photo album.

3. Encourage her to express his grief through art. Ask her to write fiction, personal essays, or poetry that expresses and identifies feelings and blockages. You can encourage artists to paint or draw. Starting a journal can be an important step for dealing with emotions.

- Ask her to try writing about the life of the person she lost.
- Alternatively, have her write about how that person has influenced her. Remind her that the deceased lives on through her.

4. Create a memory book. Memory books can help in the grieving process. Compile mementos, photos or stories about the deceased person. This helps one come to terms with the magnitude of the loss and to focus on the realities of one's new life without forgetting the lost loved one.

5. Use the open-chair technique. Place an open chair opposite the grieving person and ask her to imagine the deceased person sitting in that chair. Give the bereaved person the opportunity to speak to the person in the chair and say all the things that she would like to have said to that person.

- Playing out situations from the past or rehearsing difficult future situations may help bring closure.
- The use of objects and memorabilia, such as jewelry and other objects which the bereaved person is comfortable with, can be used to facilitate talking and bringing the mourning process to a close.

6. Don't push. Some people will want to clear their heads or process their loss before trying to commemorate their loved one. Many people have difficulty talking about what has happened. It is

your job to give the grieving party ideas about how to move on. It is not your job to force them to do something they do not want to do.

How to get a Counseling License

A counseling license is generally a requirement for mental health counselors and school counselors who wish to practice in healthcare and educational settings. Licensing requirements vary by jurisdiction and job type. Though the general educational background and many state licensing guidelines are similar, professionals seeking licensure must still research local requirements in order to choose the best academic and professional path for their career goals.

Part 1. Getting the Right Education

1. Choose the type of counseling service. Counseling is actually a large umbrella of services, and most professionals choose a specific area of expertise in which to specialize. Examples of different counseling specializations include: academic counseling, mental health counseling, substance abuse counseling, domestic or child abuse counseling, career counseling, grief counseling, marriage counseling, etc.

2. Consider your work setting. Counselors work in substance abuse clinics, hospitals, private

practices, social work facilities, schools, and universities. Deciding where you want to work can also help you determine the type of counseling you want to study.

3. Get an undergraduate degree in counseling or psychology. As an undergraduate counseling or psychology student, you can expect to study introductory courses, as well as courses heavy of statistical data and research methods. From there, you will additionally choose from upper-division courses that give you overviews of social, developmental, abnormal, and comparative psychology, which will help you in choosing a specific focus for graduate school if you haven't already decided on one. The better you do in your courses, the more options you're likely to have for graduate school.

- Your school may offer either a BA or a BS in psychology. Graduate schools do not weigh more heavily toward one or the other when reviewing applications.

4. Look for relevant extracurricular actives. Research projects, internships, and teaching assistant programs will all help you distinguish yourself when applying to graduate schools. Your department advisor can help you find available opportunities.

- Your campus may also have clubs related to psychology. Look into them and become an active member.
- Since psychology and counseling graduate programs are competitive, get as much experience under your belt as you can.

5. Take the GRE. Different institutions factor GRE scores into their applicant screening process in different ways. However, all graduate school applications for counseling programs will require that you take the GRE.

6. Apply to graduate programs. You will have to apply to psychology or counseling psychology graduate programs to earn either an MA or MS in counseling. Apply specifically to programs with a focus on the type of counseling you wish to perform as a professional. You should also apply to as many graduate schools as you can due to the highly competitive nature of the programs.

- MA programs often offer a more general approach to counseling whereas MS programs typically offer increased levels of specialization if you're already certain of the area in which you want to specialize.
- Note that an advanced degree in social work is not the same as an advanced degree in counseling. Though the two professions have some instances of crossover, the boards that govern licensing for social workers are not the same as the boards that govern counseling licenses.
- Ensure that every program to which you apply is accredited by the Council for the Accreditation of Counseling and Related Educational Programs (CACREP), the Council on Rehabilitation Education (CORE), or one of the other accrediting bodies recognized by the licensing board in your state.

7. Study hard during graduate school. Counseling programs will provide substantial clinical or hands-on experience and coursework in human behavior and development, ethics, counseling strategies, etiology of mental illness, substance abuse disorders, and other areas. Doing well in your program is going to leave you more prepared for licensing requirements.

- You may also choose to go on to receive a doctoral degree in counseling. However, this isn't necessary to get a counseling license.

8. Apply for internship and residency programs. Once you finish school, most states require you to have a certain number of hours of experience counseling in a supervised, professional environment. Look into internships and residency programs to help you start accumulating the necessary hours of experience.

Part 2. Completing Licensing Requirements for your Jurisdiction

1. Search online for state websites that outline licensing requirements. Each locality has a different set of requirements and an application process that you must follow closely.

- You can find a link to each state's guidelines to become a Licensed Professional Counselor (LPC) here.
- Study the requirements. A New York State license for mental health counselors, for example, requires good moral character, a minimum age of 21, master's degree completion,

a licensing exam, and 3,000 documented hours of post-graduate, supervised counseling experience. In addition, licensing applicants must have completed training that covers how to identify and report child abuse.

2. Speak to graduate faculty and academic counselors in your university. These professionals usually can guide you to the right licensing information and resources.

3. Study for the appropriate licensing exam. Not every state uses the same national licensing exam. However, the two most common exams are the National Counselor Examination for Licensure and Certification (NCE) and the National Clinical Mental Health Counseling Examination (NCMHCE).

- The National Board for Certified Counselors has an easy map to determine the right exam for your counseling field based on your state here.
- The NCE is the appropriate examination for the National Certified Counselor (NCC) certification. Both exams are used to determine eligibility for military health systems such as TRICARE and the Army Substance Abuse Program.
- You can find study guides as well as test prep programs for each test as well.

4. Complete the required practice hours. Most counseling license requirements include a minimum number of supervised practice hours. The actual hours and nature of the practicum varies by the type of counseling and locality.

- To become licensed as a drug and alcohol counselor in New Jersey, for example, licensing applicants must have delivered 300 hours of counseling in functions ranging from client screening and orientation to treatment planning, counseling, and crisis intervention. Many other states require as many as 3,000 hours of supervised experience via an internship or residency.

5. Take the appropriate licensing exam. Once you've met your state's supervised practice requirements, you are ready to take the appropriate exam. The length and scoring of exams varies, but the NCE, for instance, is 200 multiple choice questions. It will cover various areas, including:

- Human growth and development
- Social and cultural diversity
- Helping relationships
- Group work
- Career development
- Assessment
- Research and program evaluation
- Professional orientation and ethical practice
- Fundamental counseling issues
- Counseling process
- Diagnostic and assessment services
- Professional practice
- Professional development, supervision, and consultation.

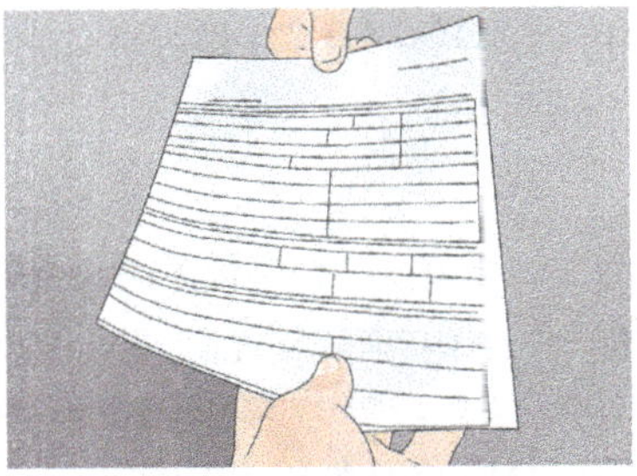

6. Submit a counseling license application. Once you've completed all the necessary pieces of your

state's specific licensing requirements, you will need to show proof to the responsible state board. Applications generally ask for documentation of academic credentials, test scores, and practice hours. In most cases, a processing fee is required.

- You can find a complete list of each state's licensing board here.
- Some states may also require you to schedule a time to appear before the board for an interview as well.

7. Maintain your counseling license by complying with local requirements. You may be required to enroll in workshops and seminars or take additional academic courses to maintain your license.

Ethics in Family Counseling

Couple and family therapy presents challenges which are often erroneously assumed to be covered under general principles about counseling and psychotherapy. A significant values difference between couple and family therapy and other mental health services is an appreciation of context, which is grounded in the foundational premise of the family as a system. This means that it is the *relationship* that is the focus of study, and all relationships are seen to exist within multiple other systems, including the therapeutic system.

Relationship issues and the values we hold about relationships are completely entwined with their social and historical context. We are constantly exposed to theories about effective relationships and relationship pathology, whether they be evidence-based or common folklore. We cannot help but be influenced by these ideas, nor by our own experience of relationships.

Competency to Practise

A core ethical responsibility to clients is the promotion of beneficence: doing good on the client's behalf. This is reflected in a number of professional areas, but starts with the therapist's competence to practise. Interestingly, couple and family therapy is quite commonly practised by therapists with little or no specific training. It seems to be thought that if one is individually trained, then it is not a great stretch to see other family members. Nothing could be further from the truth.

Issues surrounding relationships (violence and abuse, family law matters, sexual concerns, infidelity and other betrayals, severe attachment disruptions) all render this work highly complex and specialised. Without core training, duty of care is potentially breached. If you were seeking assistance for your own relationship, what qualifications would you seek in your therapist? We often provide less for our clients than we would require for ourselves.

Informed Consent

The very act of asking the initial caller to gather other family members for an appointment raises questions about the forms of 'social coercion' that this might involve. There are different levels of power and opportunity in families. One member can decide for the group, while others can be unfairly excluded from key decision making. How the therapist is positioned within this is crucial to consider. Further, there are complexities around informed consent with people across ages and circumstances, and about how one might consider sending therapeutic letters or other communications. Are the adults always the best gatekeepers for other family members? Not uncommonly, I have had children say to me that they have 'no idea' about why they are in my room, despite my parental preparation.

Confidentiality

Arranging for individual consultations within relational work raises a myriad of difficulties. While it can be important for assessing dynamics such as abuse, it also provides opportunities for disclosures that will significantly shape the work ahead. Further, issues of confidentiality and privacy are often confused, and therapists can find themselves unwittingly silenced and compromised through promises they have made in good faith. There are certain principles about moving between individual and couple or family sessions, but these are not articulated within accessible guidelines, leaving therapists to work things out on their own. It is not uncommon for well intentioned therapists to find themselves in breach of confidentiality by juggling too many agendas and finding themselves the 'fall guy'.

Neutrality and Dual Relationships

Frequently couples will ask for assistance when on a covert level they want a referee or a judgment about the behaviour of the other. Individual sessions and phone calls can be invitations to take sides, and neutrality can be called into question. There are complex issues around being engaged to 'save relationships' and then having notes subpoenaed for divorce proceedings. Besides the feelings this can evoke for the therapist, there are invitations into conflicting roles, e.g., couple/family therapist versus advocate in court.

Working with relationships involves managing multiple alliances. It is not always possible to have everyone on side at the one time. Members of the family may have conflicting or competing needs which they want equally acknowledged. Even trying to develop a focus for the work is fraught with challenges, as you question: whose voice will prevail? Improvement for one member must not occur at the expense of another.

Commonly relationship therapists will think it might be a good idea to offer individual therapy to one family member, and may well be pursued to do so by the client. This is not considered good practice, but it can be tempting to do. Really good relational work can be brought asunder by selecting/engaging in work with one member. What might be defendable reasons (not justifications) to take on individual work in this context?

The Individual Versus the Collective

Working with systems means being able to hold the relationship in mind over and above individual contributions: the notion that the sum is more than its parts. However, one still has to attend to:

- Individual responsibilities for pain and suffering, and for the stressors of addiction, mental health or family of origin trauma for example. How to address this in a relational context without pathologising one member and getting them off-side can be tricky.
- Perceived inequities in the tasks for therapy. For example, perpetrators of hurt have different tasks and responsibilities than those who have been hurt.
- Different ages and life stages
- Ensuring that safety is attended to, and knowing how to take a position when necessary, for example with mandatory reporting.

Further important issues in the field which involve specialised ethical and practice considerations include:

- The perennial question of working with whoever can come to sessions or insisting that all must attend sessions
- Working effectively and respectfully with culturally diverse clients and communities
- Working with gay and lesbian clients and same-sex parents .

Interventions and Case Management

Couple and family therapy has advanced different models of practice. Over time, therapeutic strategies (e.g., use of paradox, strategic manoeuvres, prescriptions, triangulation) have been critically analysed in terms of how much stress is acceptable in achieving change and a post modern framework has been adopted as more respectful. In terms of our role, while we may have preferences for *therapeutic* intervention, we have to be prepared to also be advocates, to take positions (on abuse and violence for example) and to be strategic in our case management. We need to enhance growth and positive relationships, not act as social control agents or gatekeepers of community values not in keeping with the client's own.

How to Maintain Confidentiality in Counseling

Confidentiality is an essential part of the counseling relationship. A client must be able to trust that the personal information he or she shares with you will not be revealed to other people. To protect their professional relationships, a counselor must explain the benefits and problems inherent in counseling services and clarify the limits of confidentiality to the client. Importantly, counselors have their own set of professional obligations which vary slightly from those of other mental health providers and which will vary from state to state.

Method 1. Explaining Confidentiality

1. Provide informed consent. To give informed consent, the counselor must explain the benefits and risks of counseling as well as its alternatives. They must also explain state laws regarding when they may be required to break confidentiality and describe how they might be required to do so. The counselor must request permission to record counseling sessions in writing or via video and audio. Counselors have a wide range of issues they should raise during a discussion of informed consent.

- These include the purposes, goals, techniques, and limitations of counseling.
- The counselors should discuss their qualifications, their credentials, their relevant experience, their approach to counseling and provisions for continuation of service should the counselor become unavailable to continue treatment.
- You should also explain fees, billing, and procedures in case of nonpayment.
- If any supervisors or peers will review records, this should be noted in the informed consent procedure.

2. Explain protection procedures. To obtain informed consent you need to explain how you will protect confidentiality. This includes detailing how records will be stored. It also includes explaining cases in which the client's comments are not confidential.

- This applies to electronic communications as well, including after hour phone calls, text messages, email, and skype sessions. You should discuss how confidentiality shall be maintained in such circumstances, and what risks to client confidentiality emerge when you are contacted after hours.

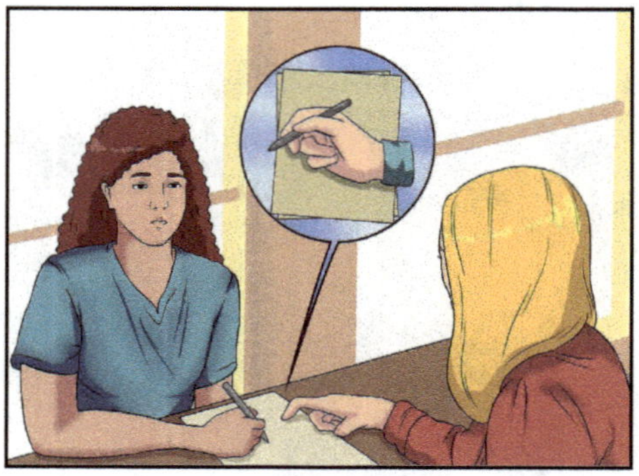

3. Give the patient a form to sign. You should provide a written form for the patient to sign, authorizing informed consent. This should remain in your patient's file. The language of the form is subject to change, but it should be inviting and easy to read. It should also cover most of the aforementioned points.

- It is advisable that you keep a copy of the form in the lobby so that patients can read it before speaking to you.

4. Get parental permission for minors. When counseling those under 18, informed consent must come from a parent. You should have two separate forms, one informed consent form that the minor signs and another consent for treatment of minors form that the parent signs.

5. Describe research. If the sessions will be the basis for published research, this should be disclosed

to the patient. Whether or not they will be anonymous and how their anonymity will be protected must be discussed.

Method 2. Protecting Client Records

1. Store records safely. To maintain confidentiality, it is the counselor's responsibility to keep the client's records safe and appropriately secured. Records should be locked away where only the counselor can reach them.

2. Protect records at home. It is important that you lock away documents at home as well as at the office. However, you might need to step away from your desk or take an emergency phone call with others around. You should ensure that anyone you reside with is aware of confidentiality procedures.

- You should inform anyone with whom you reside what areas are off limits.
- You should also make it clear to anyone around when a phone call is confidential. Close the door and inform them that they should leave you alone.

3. Provide records to client. A client may request his or her own records in most situations. The

counselor however can refuse to provide access to portions of the records if it will cause harm to the client. The counselor must document the request of the client and the reason for withholding the information.

- When there are multiple clients, such as with family counseling, then the counselor should only provide records relevant to the individual client, not other clients in the group.

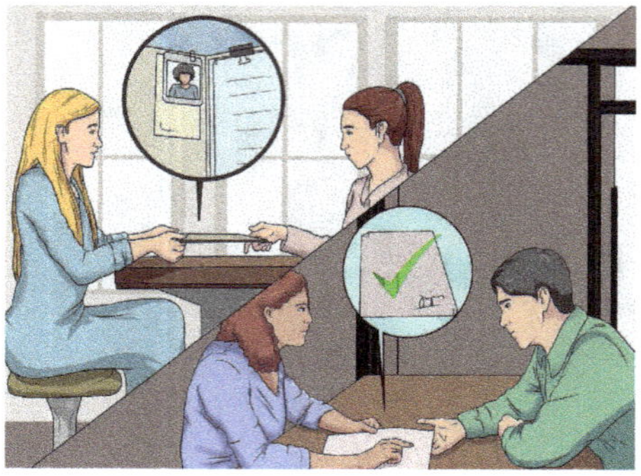

4. Do not release records to any third parties. A client's records are only to be released to a third party if the client has provided written consent. This includes third parties who pay for treatment.

- With minors it is important to also obtain consent from parents before releasing information to a third party.

5. Be aware of exceptions. There are some exceptions when confidentiality should not be preserved. These vary somewhat with state law. You should make both yourself and your clients aware of these exceptions. Generally there are a few standards for the lapse of confidentiality:

- Confidentiality is waived when the client makes threats of suicide or homicide.
- It is also waived when information is disclosed relevant to the abuse of children or the elderly.
- Depending on the state in which you operate, you might be required to reveal to a third party when your client has a life-threatening disease that could be communicated to said third party.
- If a court subpoenas your records you should ask for written consent from your client. If that is not forthcoming, it is your responsibility to try to limit or prevent the disclosure of records.

6. Stay current with counseling ethics and regulations. Counseling associations such as the American Association of Marriage and Family Therapists (AAMFT), the American Counseling Association (ACA)and the American Mental Health Counselors Association (AMHCA) all provide their members with a set of ethics for conducting counseling which include how to maintain confidentiality in a therapeutic relationship. You should also familiarize yourself with state regulations.

- When a counselor finds him or herself in a situation where maintaining a client's confidentiality becomes a problem, consulting with colleagues and/or a direct supervisor can help the counselor with appropriate decision-making.
- A counselor may also discuss confidentiality concerns with his or her own therapist, so long as they don't reveal information that may identify the client being discussed.

Method 3. Protecting Against Lapses in Conversations

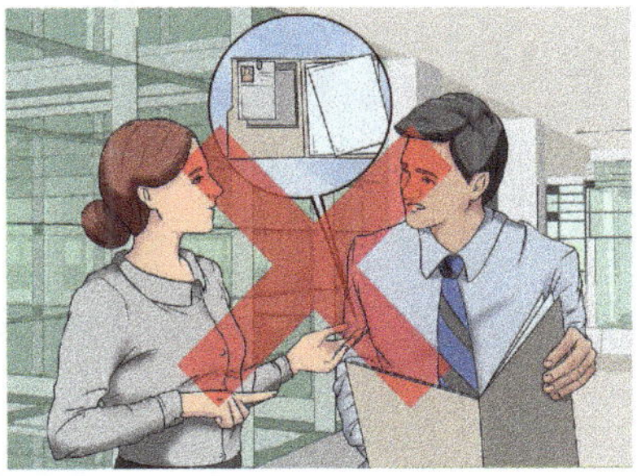

1. Avoid confidential details in discussions with peers. When a counselor seeks advice from a fellow professional about a client, they should not disclose confidential information. Information that is provided should not allow for the identification of the client. Furthermore, it should be limited to what is necessary to obtain relevant suggestions.

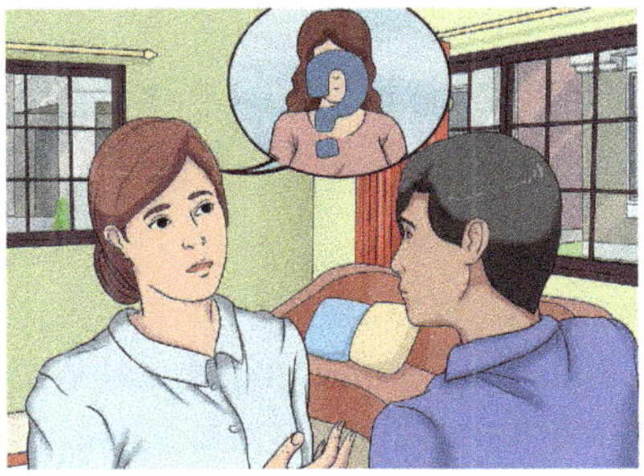

2. Change details. When engaged in conversation with friends or family, change important information about clients. Alter facts so that the client will be in no way identifiable.

3. Do not engage in conversations in public. All conversations about clients should be in a private setting. If you receive an urgent phone call from a client, try to find a private place from which to return the call.

4. Do not acknowledge clients in public. Clients might not want their association with you to be public knowledge. Do not acknowledge them, unless they acknowledge you first.

How to Deal with Lesbian, Gay and Bisexual Clients

Guideline 1. Psychologists strive to be knowledgeable about and respect the importance of lesbian, gay, and bisexual relationships.

Lesbian, gay, and bisexual couples are both similar to and different from heterosexual couples. They form relationships for similar reasons, express similar satisfactions with their relationships, and follow developmental patterns similar to heterosexual couples. The differences are derived from several factors, including different patterns of sexual behavior, gender role socialization, and the stigmatizing of their relationships.

Same-sex couples must sometimes adapt to conditions that are hostile to or devalue their relationships. These include the psychological effects of political campaigns against same-sex marriage and the prohibition of legal and medical protections for same-sex families as in Virginia and Florida. Furthermore, relationship patterns and choices among lesbian, gay, and bisexual individuals may be affected by early-life stigma and marginalization.

Changes in physical health may present unique stressors, especially to older lesbian, gay, and bisexual couples (e.g., possible separation from partners, possible loss of contact for partners in nursing homes or other inpatient settings, facing homophobia in caretakers or fellow residents in nursing homes and assisted living situations). Lesbian, gay, and bisexual clients may have become so inured to the effects of stigma and discrimination in their relationships that they may not recognize the contribution of stigma to the conflicts they face.

The relationship structures of lesbian, gay, and bisexual couples vary and may present unique concerns. Non-monogamous or polyamorous relationships may be more common and more acceptable among gay men and bisexual individuals than is typical for lesbians or heterosexuals. In addition, many lesbians and gay men come out years after they have been heterosexually married.

Application

Psychologists are encouraged to consider the negative effects of societal prejudice and discrimination on lesbian, gay, and bisexual relationships. A couple may not recognize the contribution of stigma and marginalization to the common relationship problems that all couples may encounter. Nonetheless, lesbian, gay, and bisexual couples may seek therapy for reasons similar to those of heterosexual couples (e.g., communication difficulties, sexual problems, dual career issues, and commitment decisions) or for dissimilar reasons (e.g., disclosure of sexual orientation; differences between partners in the disclosure process; and issues derived from the effects of gender socialization). For example, when one partner has disclosed his sexual orientation to family of origin and the other has not, the pair may encounter conflicts around where to spend the holidays, or whether to "de-gay" the house when visitors are expected. Psychologists are therefore encouraged to consider familial and other social and cultural factors in conducting therapy with lesbian, gay and bisexual couples.

Familiarity with non-traditional relationship structures may be helpful to the psychologist working with same-sex couples. Some gay, lesbian, and bisexual couples may need to resolve ambiguity in areas of commitment and boundaries, cope with homophobia, and develop adequate social supports. Monogamy is a normative expectation in many heterosexual relationships, whereas it is not always assumed among gay male couples.

The relationships of lesbian, gay, and bisexual individuals are diverse. In the absence of socially sanctioned supports for their relationships, lesbian, gay, and bisexual people create their own relationship models and support systems. It is useful for psychologists to be aware of the diversity of these relationships and refrain from applying a heterosexist model when working with lesbian, gay and bisexual couples. This may be particularly salient with respect to the sexual lives of lesbian, gay, and bisexual couples. Healthy sexual expression is generally taken to be an element of overall relationship satisfaction. It is helpful for psychologists working with lesbian, gay, and bisexual couples to be sensitized to and knowledgeable about common sexual practices and concerns shared by lesbian, gay, and bisexual couples (e.g., sexual frequency, various forms of sexual dysfunction, concerns related to intimacy and desire). Psychologists are encouraged to recognize that internalized heterosexism can complicate the development of healthy sexual relationships. Psychologists are also encouraged to recognize the particular challenges that men and women in heterosexual marriages face in coming out and integrating their lesbian, gay, or bisexual orientation into their lives. In addition, the spouses and families of these individuals may require therapeutic support.

Guideline 2. Psychologists strive to understand the experiences and challenges faced by lesbian, gay, and bisexual parents.

Research has indicated that lesbian, gay, and bisexual parents are as capable as heterosexual parents. In fact, Flaks, Ficher, Masterpasqua, and Joseph found that lesbian couples had stronger parenting awareness skills than heterosexual couples. Bos, van Balen, and van den Boom reported that lesbian social mothers (non-biological mothers) had higher quality parent-child interactions, were more committed as parents, and were more effective in childrearing when compared to fathers in heterosexual marriages. Such findings are important to note, given the context of discrimination that lesbian, gay, and bisexual parents face (e.g., legal barriers to foster parenting, same-sex and second-parent adoption, the threat of loss of custody of children, prohibitions against living with one's same-sex partner, and the lack of legal rights of one of the parents). In becoming parents, lesbian, gay, and bisexual people face challenges not required of heterosexual people, such as stressors related to alternative insemination and surrogacy. Other unique concerns for lesbian, gay, and bisexual parents include lack of support from families and friends, and homophobic reactions from pediatricians, daycare providers, and school personnel. Families of the non-biological lesbian mother may be resistant to seeing nonbiological children as true grandchildren/nieces/nephews.

Increasingly, research has focused on the children of lesbian, gay, and bisexual parents. Three main concerns have been raised (primarily by those in the legal and social welfare systems) with regard to the well-being of children raised by lesbian, gay, and bisexual parents. These include: (1) the gender identification, gender role behavior, and sexual orientation of the children; (2) the personal development of the children; and (3) the social experiences of such children. Patterson (2005) conducted a comprehensive review of the literature in each of these areas. Her review of the empirical data (primarily based on children of lesbian mothers) indicated that none of these areas of concern has merit. Patterson also reported that the data showed no major differences between children reared by lesbian parents in contrast to those raised by heterosexual mothers with regard to personal development in such areas as self-esteem, locus of control, intelligence, behavior problems, personality, school adjustment, and psychiatric health. In light of research findings supporting the positive outcomes for children of lesbian and gay parents, the American Academy of Pediatrics released a statement in 2002 supporting second-parent adoption in lesbian, gay, and bisexual households.

Application

APA "encourages psychologists to act to eliminate all discrimination based on sexual orientation in matters of adoption, child custody and visitation, foster care, and reproductive health services". While bias and misinformation continue to exist in the educational, legal, and social welfare systems, psychologists also are urged to correct this misinformation in their work with parents, children, community organizations, and institutions and to provide accurate information based upon scientifically and professionally derived knowledge. Psychologists strive to recognize the challenges faced by lesbian, gay, and bisexual parents and are encouraged to explore these issues with their clients. For example, denial of access to marriage creates barriers for same-sex parents in accessing the same legal and economic benefits and social status as married heterosexual couples. At the same time, psychologists are urged to recognize the unique strengths and resilience of lesbian, gay, and bisexual families. Psychologists are encouraged to examine the various facets of identity (e.g., race and ethnicity, culture, socioeconomic class, disability, religious or spiritual traditions) that intersect in creating the experiences of lesbian, gay, and bisexual parents.

Guideline 3. Psychologists recognize that the families of lesbian, gay, and bisexual people may include people who are not legally or biologically related.

For a significant number of lesbian, gay, and bisexual individuals, nondisclosure of sexual orientation and/or lack of acknowledgement of their intimate relationships may result in emotional distancing from their family of origin. Even when families are accepting, this acceptance often may be tolerance rather than true acceptance. For many lesbian, gay, and bisexual people, a network of close friends may constitute an alternative family structure—one that may not be based on legal and/or biological relationships. These families of choice provide social connections and familial context for lesbian, gay, and bisexual individuals and may be more significant than the individual's family of origin. Such family structures can mitigate the effects of discrimination and the absence of legal or institutional recognition.

Application

Given the importance of social support in relationship satisfaction, stigma management, and psychological well-being, psychologists are encouraged to recognize and value lesbian, gay, and bisexual family structures. Psychologists also are urged to consider the stress that clients may experience when their families of origin, employers, or others do not recognize their alternative family structures. When working with lesbian, gay, and bisexual clients, it can be helpful to ask the client about his/her friendship network, the quality of his/her relationships in that network, and if he/she considers members of this network to be "family." A related issue would be the person's level of involvement with the lesbian, gay, and bisexual community, as connection with the community may provide the individual with role models, social support, a sense of solidarity, and other resources helpful in the development of a positive identity.

Guideline 4. Psychologists strive to understand the ways in which a person's lesbian, gay, or bisexual orientation may have an impact on his or her family of origin and the relationship with that family of origin.

There are many responses a family can have upon learning that one of its members is lesbian, gay, or bisexual. Some families of origin may be unprepared to accept a lesbian, gay, or bisexual child or family member because of familial, ethnic, or cultural norms; religious beliefs; or negative stereotypes. For these families, this awareness may precipitate a family crisis that can result in profound distancing from or expulsion of the lesbian, gay, or bisexual family member, rejection of the parents and siblings by that family member, parental guilt and self-recrimination, or conflicts within the parents' relationship. On the other hand, there are families of origin in which acceptance of their lesbian, gay, or bisexual member is unconditional or without crisis. Research does suggest, however, that even supportive families may experience an adjustment period upon learning that a family member is lesbian, gay, or bisexual.

Bisexual individuals may experience some unique complications with their families of origin. Persons who identify as bisexual and become romantically involved with same-sex partners may receive pressure from their families of origin to choose a partner of the other gender and bisexuals who are in mixed-sex relationships may have difficulty maintaining their bisexual identity within their family of origin and extended family.

Some young adult life transitions (e.g., choosing careers, deciding to parent) will be particularly complicated for the lesbian, gay, or bisexual family member. It may be challenging to explain to family members how sexual orientation and experiences related to stigma may impact decisions related to work and career, sexual and romantic relationships, and parenting (Patterson, 2007). Both the family of origin and the extended family may grapple with the recognition of same-sex partners and children raised by a same-sex couple.

Application

Psychologists are encouraged to explore with lesbian, gay, and bisexual clients any issues and concerns related to their family of origin and extended family. Psychologists strive to understand the culturally specific risks of coming out to one's family of origin. For example, racial and ethnic minority families may fear losing the support of their community if they are open about having a lesbian, gay, or bisexual child. Psychologists can assist clients in facilitating discussions with their families about their identities as well as about cultural stigma. Families may need support in developing new understandings of sexual orientation, confronting the ways in which negative societal attitudes about homosexuality and bisexuality are manifested within the family, and supporting family members in addressing difficulties related to societal stigmatization.

Newer models of family therapy move beyond addressing difficulties and promote processes of creating constructive systemic change. Psychologists are encouraged to assist families in developing long-term support for their lesbian, gay, and bisexual members and to monitor the relationships among family members beyond the adjustment to discovering the identity of a lesbian, gay, or bisexual member. Psychologists are urged to assist lesbian, gay, and bisexual clients in their efforts to present accurate information regarding sexual orientation to their families. Finally, psychologists strive to be aware of the cultural variations in a family's reaction and ways of adapting to a lesbian, gay, or bisexual member. Local and national resources are available that can provide information, assistance, and support to family members.

How to Guide Clients to Heal from Childhood Trauma

1. Ground it.

For this process to work, you must be in your body and in the now. To begin, find a quiet place where you won't be disturbed. Sit comfortably with your eyes closed, and take several deep breaths, bringing your awareness into your body. Squeeze and release your muscles, and feel the heaviness in your arms. Let yourself feel connected to the ground under you. Imagine a stream of energy going from your tailbone all the way down into the center of the earth. Once you feel that you are centered in your body, go to Step 2.

2. Recall it.

Think of a situation that you've been upset about recently. Find something that provoked a mild to strong emotional reaction, or that would have if you didn't feel emotionally numb. Review what happened in as much detail as possible, and imagine yourself back in that time and place. Experience it all again with your senses. When emotions begin to arise, go to Step 3.

3. Sense it.

Continue breathing deeply, and spend a moment in quiet relaxation. Then, mentally scan your body for any sensations. I call this process "percolating" because of the way your emotions will stir and bubble up inside you. Observe any physical response you experience – tingling, tightness, burning, etc. Each of these sensations is a bit of information you need to understand your past experience. Explore these sensations, and silently describe them to yourself in as much detail as you can. Once you've explored and described all of your physical reactions, you can move on to Step 4.

4. Name it.

Associate an emotion with each of the sensations you feel. Is the tightness in your chest anxiety? Is the heat you feel traveling up your arms anger? Before starting this exercise, you may want to print out this list of emotions you can find this list on the bottom right side of the page. It's important to recognize the often subtle distinctions between sometimes similar emotions. This will give you a greater sense of your experience and a richer knowledge of yourself. Once you've named your emotions, go to Step 5.

5. Love it.

As part of a mindful approach to healing from trauma, we need to fully accept everything that we feel. Whether it's true to your conscious mind at this moment or not, say, "I love myself for feeling (angry, sad, anxious, etc.)." Do this with every emotion you feel, especially the harder ones. Embrace your humanness, and love yourself for it. After you've accepted and loved yourself for each of your emotions, you can move on to Step 6.

6. Feel and experience it.

Sit with your emotions and their sensations, letting the feelings percolate and flow. Don't try to change or hide them; observe them. Acknowledge and welcome any discomfort you feel, knowing it will be gone soon and will help you to heal. Let your body respond the way it wants or needs to. If you feel the urge to cry, cry. If you feel the need to yell something or punch something, you should yell or punch the air. Expressing your emotions — in a productive way — is key to getting them moving inside you and to fully process them. When you've fully felt and experienced your emotions, move to Step 7.

7. Receive its message and wisdom.

Do the sensations or emotions you're experiencing right now connect with one or more experiences in your past? Do they give you any insight into the root of the trauma or a negative, limiting belief about yourself? Right now, you might be thinking, "I'm not getting anything." Ask yourself: "If this sensation or emotion were going to say something to me, what would it be?" If you still have trouble, do some free writing. Journal about what the feeling means, for a full 10 minutes without stopping. When you think you've heard all the messages your emotions are sending you, move on to Step 8.

8. Share it.

If you feel comfortable sharing your reflections with someone else, do that. Otherwise, write about them on your own. Describe what happened when the wounding incident first occurred, how you reacted at the time, and what you've come to see about it now. Talking or writing about your experiences and emotions is an important step in healing. Writing letters (but not sending them) to those who hurt you can be a very effective method for moving an emotion out of your system. Once you've shared your reflections.

9. Let it go.

Visualize the energy your trauma took up inside you leaving your body, or perform a ritual of physical release, like (safely) burning a letter you've written to the person who hurt you, or casting off the trauma in the form of an object into the sea. You can borrow a ritual from Judaism called Tashlikh. During the period of repentance, many Jews cast off their sins into a natural, flowing body of water in the form of breadcrumbs. Instead of sins, you can cast off traumas and the emotions and sensations that go with them.

Crisis Intervention Counselor

Crisis intervention counselors are trained mental health professionals who help people in distress. They might counsel people in danger of harming themselves or others; support those undergoing acute crises, such as terror attacks or natural disasters; and help clients dealing with other distressing issues, such as grief, loss and bereavement. Crisis counselors work in various settings, including telephone crisis counseling centers, schools, mental health clinics and humanitarian aide organizations.

Assessment

In many cases, crisis counselors conduct face-to-face assessments with clients in their natural settings to determine their specific needs. Telephone crisis counselors may perform brief assessments over the phone. Clients in crisis may require immediate referral to medical services, assistance with concrete needs, such as food and clothing, or they may be in a state of psychological shock and require psychiatric intervention. Crisis counselors usually meet with clients on individual, couples or family bases to perform assessments. In some cases, they may also meet with groups to perform group assessments, such as in cases of community crises.

Counseling

Crisis intervention is a short-term form of treatment to help clients deal with the immediate aftermath of a crisis situation. In most situations, counselors provide brief counseling services to help individuals and communities regain a sense of safety, return to their normal level of functioning and to prevent psychological disorders such as post-traumatic stress disorder, or PTSD. Crisis intervention is not intended to replace long-term counseling or psychological and psychiatric treatment. Crisis counselors usually counsel clients for brief periods of time to provide support and to encourage survivors to discuss their experiences.

Advocacy

Clients in crisis often enter a state of psychological shock and withdrawal as a way of handling the aftermath of the disaster or crisis situation. They may be momentarily unable to arrange for their immediate needs. A crisis counselor may provide temporary forms of advocacy to help clients meet these needs. This may include explaining client needs to service providers or helping clients apply for social services. But the ultimate goal of a crisis counselor is to help her clients regain sufficient levels of functioning so that they are able to resume advocating for themselves.

Referral

Providing accurate and timely referrals is another important responsibility of many crisis counselors. Crisis counselors often do not have the time, resources or expertise to assist clients with certain needs, such as psychiatric services or housing. They must be well-informed about community resources and different types of governmental assistance available to survivors of certain crisis situations.

How to Become a Crisis Intervention Counselor

Education

You can become a counselor with a bachelor's degree in sociology, psychology, social work, counseling or another related field. You can also enter the profession through divinity school degrees as they include counseling in their curriculum.

Most states do not require certification, but if you have the education to qualify otherwise, you might consider becoming certified through one of several organizations that offer this service. Usually you will have to take a certification program. In this programme these courses are included:

- Crisis Intervention Theory—This includes the ethical and cultural issues that affect trauma.
- Crisis Intervention Assessment and Treatment I and II —This is a study of current factors and issued related to determining the types and level of crisis the client faces.
- Clinical Stress Management—In this course you will learn concepts and methods of stress management.
- Relaxation Strategies—This is a class that teaches the anatomy of the central nervous system and discusses how breathing affects stress and tension.
- Crisis Intervention Treatment Planning—In this course you learn how to combine your assessment with treatment goals and work with other professionals to reach those goals.

The program, offered here as an example, requires that applicants have a bachelor's degree in psychology, social work, sociology or a health-related field or that they are a licensed social worker, counselor or healthcare worker currently employed in their profession. Other acceptable applicants are those employed in criminal justice, EMTs or those currently employed in disaster response.

How to Deal with a Bipolar Family Member using Cognitive Behavioral Therapy Techniques

Behavioral Experiments

In Cognitive Behavioral Therapy, behavioral experiments are designed to test thoughts. Example: You might do a behavioral experiment to test the thought "If I criticize myself after overeating, I'll overeat less" vs. "If I talk to myself kindly after overeating, I'll overeat less."

To do this you would try each approach on different occasions and monitor your subsequent overeating. This would give you objective feedback about whether self-criticism or self-kindness was more effective in reducing future overeating. This type of behavioral experiment might also help counteract a thought like "If I'm kind to myself, it's like giving myself a free pass to overeat and I'll lose all self-control." (CBT Behavioral experiment example)

Thought Records

Like behavioral experiments, thought records are also designed to test the validity of thoughts. For example, a clinical psychology student who gets negative feedback from a supervisor might jump to the conclusion "My supervisor thinks I'm useless." The student could do a thought record evaluating the evidence for and against that thought. Evidence against the thought might be things like "My supervisor gave me positive feedback yesterday" or "My supervisor is allowing me to run assessments and give feedback to clients. If she thought I was useless, she probably wouldn't be allowing me to feedback to clients."

Once you've looked at the objective evidence for and against a thought side by side, the idea is to come up with several more balanced thoughts. An example of a balanced thought might be "I made a mistake in doing. Making mistakes is normal. I can learn from this. My supervisor will be impressed to see me learning from my mistakes and incorporating her feedback." Thought records tend to help change beliefs on a logical level, whereas behavioral experiments may be more helpful in also changing beliefs on a gut or felt level i.e., what you emotionally feel is true, regardless of the objective evidence. (CBT Thought record example)

Pleasant Activity Scheduling

Pleasant activity scheduling is a surprisingly effective Cognitive Behavioral Therapy technique. It's particularly helpful for depression.

Try this: write the next seven days down on a piece of paper, starting with today (e.g., Thurs, Fri, Sat). For each day, schedule one pleasant activity (anything you enjoy that's not unhealthy) that you wouldn't normally do. It could be as simple as reading a chapter of a novel or eating your lunch away from your desk without rushing.

An alternative version of this technique is to also schedule an activity a day that gives you a sense of mastery, competence, or accomplishment. Again, choose something small that you wouldn't usually do. Aim for something that will take you less than ten minutes.

An advanced version of this technique would be to schedule three pleasant activities per day - one for sometime during your morning, one for the afternoon, and one for evening.

Doing activities that produce higher levels of positive emotions in your daily life will help make your thinking less negative, narrow, rigid, and self-focused.

Situation Exposure Hierarchies

Situation exposure hierarchies involve putting things you would normally avoid on a list. For example, a client with an eating disorder might make a list of forbidden foods, with ice cream at the top of the list and full fat yogurt near the bottom. A client with social anxiety might put asking someone on a date at the top of her list and asking a woman for directions near the bottom of her list. For each item on your list, rate how distressed you think you'd be if you did it. Use a scale from 0-10. For example, ice-cream = 10, full fat yogurt = 2. Order your list from highest to lowest. The theme of the list should reflect your problem.

Try to have several items at each distress number so there are no big jumps. The idea is to work your way through the list from lowest to highest. You would likely experiment with each item several times over a period of a few days until the distress you feel about being in that situation is about half of what it was the first time you tried it (e.g., you can eat full fat yogurt with only 1/10 distress instead of 2/10). Then move to the next item up the list.

Imagery Based Exposure

One version of imagery exposure involves bringing to mind a recent memory that provoked strong negative emotions. For example, let's take the earlier example of a clinical psychology student being given critical feedback by a supervisor. In imagery exposure, the person would bring the situation of being given the feedback to mind and remember it in lots of sensory detail (e.g., the supervisor's tone of voice, what the room looked like). They would also attempt to accurately label the emotions and thoughts they experienced during the interaction, and what their behavioral urges were (e.g., to run out of the room and cry, or to get angry). In prolonged imagery exposure, the person would keep visualizing the image in detail until their level of distress reduced to about half its initial level (say from 8/10 to 4/10).

Imagery based exposure can help counteract rumination because it helps make intrusive painful memories less likely to trigger rumination. Because of this, it also tends to help reduce avoidance coping. When a person is less distressed by intrusive memories they're able to choose healthier coping actions.

Techniques and Exercises of Family Counseling

2

Family therapy requires a range of counseling methods and techniques such as structural therapy, narrative therapy, transgenerational therapy, strategic therapy, relationship counseling and education, etc. This chapter explores the techniques and exercises of family counseling for guiding clients in building better relationship, using art and play-based activities, creating a genogram, using genograms for psychotherapy, etc.

Exercises and Techniques

If family therapy sounds like a treatment that would benefit you and your loved ones, the best course of action is to find a licensed professional with whom you can build a good working relationship and address the problems your family is facing. However, if you're not quite ready for this step or there are obstacles between you and getting treatment, there are many exercises and suggestions that you may find to be a good alternative.

The exercises and techniques below are meant to be used within the context of a therapeutic working relationship, but some also have applications for those who wish to explore the possibilities of family therapy before committing to a long-term treatment with a therapist. If you are a therapist or other mental health professional, you may find these exercises to be useful additions to your therapy toolbox.

How to Guide your Client to Build Better Relationship

1. Create a New Memory. As the saying goes, "actions speak louder than words". To "speak" loudly about your intention to build better relationships, make a brand new memory together. A new adventure can start at your neighborhood park. It can also be as simple as cooking together, taking a walk, or reading a book.

Creating a new positive memory will not only renew bond between you and your family members it will give you something to talk about, for days or even years to come.

2. Make an Art Project. A great art project that's easy and fun for children and teens are collages.

Collages are an easy project to do even for individuals that do not consider themselves to be good artists.

Using markers, crayons, pictures, and cut outs, encourage your child to make an "All About Me" collage. You can even do one and share them with each other. Other art projects can include a "Then" collage from the past, or a "Future" collage for what they would like to be in 1, 5, or 10 years. Making collages together is a great way to not only have fun, but look at common interests and goals for your family while incorporating each family member in an activity.

3. Toss Around a Ball. One of my most used tools is my "emotions ball", which like it sounds, is a ball that has different emotions written on it ranging from "joyful" to "lonely" to "silly". Tossing this ball around can start a conversation about emotions in many different ways.

Teenagers are often relieved to have something to do while talking about feelings and younger children simply enjoy the physical activity. Emotions can be brought in to the conversation by asking each member to describe a time they felt a certain emotion every time they catch the ball. Participants can also be asked to act out an emotion.

There are a variety of ways this ball can be used to fit your family. Some families have chosen to make their own emotions ball at home by writing on a beach ball – a great idea to use things you might have in your house already. Talking about emotions can start new conversations and sharing with each other will help develop trust and understanding between family members.

4. Play Board Games. Yes, even simple board or card games can be a therapy tool, used to start creating new connections and strengthen bonds between family members. One of my favorite games for family therapy is "Go Fish". This is a simple card game that allows for lots of conversation to happen while you're playing. However, at home, even more elaborate games that require more concentration will help create new positive memories. This time spent together without other distractions will open up the opportunity to build your relationship.

The Miracle Question

This exercise can be used in individual, couples, or family therapy, and is intended to help the client(s) explore the type of future they would like to build. We all struggle at times, but sometimes the struggle is greater because we simply do not know what our goals actually are.

The Miracle Question is an excellent way to help the client or clients probe their own dreams and desires. When used in the context of couples or family therapy, it can aid clients in understanding what they significant other or family member needs in order to be happy with their relationship.

The Miracle Question is a goal setting question that is useful when a client simply does not know what a preferred future would look like. It can be used with individuals to set the course for therapy, with couples, to clarify what each person needs from each other and with families, who too often see one person as the culprit. By using the Miracle Question and asking each person what a better life would look like, the system sees perhaps for the first time, what others need from each other.

What does It Look Like

"Suppose tonight, while you slept, a miracle occurred. When you awake tomorrow, what would be some of the things you would notice that would tell you life had suddenly gotten better?"

The therapist stays with the question even if the client describes an "impossible" solution, such as a deceased person being alive, and acknowledges that wish and then asks "how would that make a difference in your life?" Then as the client describes that he/she might feel as if they have their companion back, again, the therapist asks "how would that make a difference?" With that, the client may say, "I would have someone to confide in and support me." From there, the therapist would ask the client to think of others in the client's life who could begin to be a confidant in a very small manner.

How does it Help The Client?

It catapults the client from a problem saturated context into a visionary context where he/she has a moment of freedom, to step out of the problem story and into a story where they are more problem free. But, more importantly, it helps the therapist to know exactly what the client wants from therapy and this is what makes Solution Focused Therapy so efficient and brief.

The Miracle Question as a Cool Intervention

It helps the therapist see where the client wants to go. Too often, therapists assume that a client needs to grieve, leave their spouse, quit their job, after the client describes why he/she has come to therapy. The Miracle Question helps the client and therapist to address exactly what the client wants, not what the therapist thinks is best.

How to use Art and Play-based Activities in Family Therapy

There are several compelling reasons for using art and play when working with children in the context of the family. Eliana Gil, one of the pioneers of family play therapy, emphasizes that "play techniques can engage parents and children in enhanced communication, understanding, and emotional relatedness, and can assist clinicians in their important work, and thus should be considered a viable and pivotal part of the family therapy work". Similarly, Bailey and Sori aptly put it, "Family play therapy moves treatment from the intellectual, cerebral, abstract world familiar to adults, to the world of imagination, spontaneity, metaphor, and creativity that is familiar to children". Family play therapy "lives in the twilight zone between cognition and emotion, where the defenses are not on the alert".

Art therapy is also an effective technique with families because "it bypasses those censors that families may have adeptly construed. A family that did not know how to express feelings directly may find a way to do so when given an opportunity to draw or paint". When family members engage in an arts or play-based therapeutic activity, they often express thoughts and feelings that they otherwise may not feel comfortable expressing through traditional family talk therapy. Art and play-based activities can unlock a deeper level of communication.

Play and arts therapies differ from traditional "talk therapy" in that they engage emotions in a direct and physical way, generate creative energy as a healing force, and creatively enable clients to express their problems and conflicts.

Engaging The Family in Play and Art Activities

Parents may have difficulty understanding the rationale and effectiveness of using play and art techniques in family therapy sessions. They may view games, drawings, and puppets merely as sources of entertainment for children. Parents may also feel uncomfortable, embarrassed, or silly participating in playful family therapy. It is helpful to meet with parents prior to the first family session to explain the value of using play and art activities in family therapy and to help them embrace this approach. Wark outlines the following instructions for the parent session:

1. Inform parents that play and art activities are a part of your family therapy approach. Give examples of the techniques that are usually incorporated into sessions, such as games, drawings, and puppets. Ask the parents for their reaction to this method of working. If the parents express doubt or discomfort with this approach, normalize their feelings.
2. Ask the parents for their image and expectations of therapy, i.e., "What are your ideas of how therapy should be conducted with families? What do you think would help your children feel comfortable in therapy? Do you think it will be easy or difficult for your children to talk directly and openly about their thoughts and feelings? Do you think your children will be able to sit still during the entire session? What would help your children participate in the sessions?"
3. Explain some of the key benefits of using play and art techniques in family therapy: (a) children enjoy games, drawing, and using puppets, therefore they will feel comfortable with a play-based approach; (b) since children communicate through play, they will be able to express themselves more easily than traditional "talk therapy"; (c) since play and art activities are active in nature, children's attention is more likely to be captivated and sustained for the duration of the session; and (d) research shows that play helps children develop cognitive, affective, and sensorimotor skills.

When introducing play and art interventions into family sessions, “it is helpful to begin with activities that guarantee success; these tasks should be easy and should not require an explicit finished product. In addition, if the family members are asked to work as a group or in pairs, they may feel less conscious of their own contribution”.

Colored Candy Go Around

If you’re looking for a fun and creative icebreaker or introduction to family therapy, this exercise can be a great way to start.

To engage in this exercise with your family, you need a package of Skittles, M&Ms, or a similar colorful candy. Distribute seven pieces to each family member, and instruct them to sort their candy by color (and refraining from eating it just yet.).

Next, ask a family member to pick a color and share how many they have. For however many candies of this color they have, instruct them to give the same number of responses to the following prompts based on the color:

- Green – words to describe your family
- Purple – ways your family has fun
- Orange – things you would like to improve about your family
- Red – things you worry about
- Yellow – favorite memories with your family

When the first family member has given their answers, tell them to choose the next family member to answer the same prompt based on the number of candies that person has. Once the prompt has been answered, the candies can be eaten.

When all family members have responded to these prompts, initiate a discussion based on the answers provided by the family. The following questions can facilitate discussion:

1. What did you learn?
2. What was the most surprising thing you learned about someone else?
3. How will you work towards making changes/improvements?

Emotions Ball

This is a simple exercise, requiring only a ball and a pen or marker to write with. You may even recognize it, as it is frequently used with children and teenagers in many contexts, as it takes the pressure off of talking about emotions for those who may be uncomfortable sharing their feelings.

A beach ball is a perfect ball for this activity, as it is big enough to write several emotions on and it is easy to throw back and forth in a circle. Write several emotions on the ball, such as "joyful," "lonely," "silly," or "sad."

Gather your family into a circle and begin to toss the ball back and forth between family members. When a family member catches the ball, have them describe a time when they felt the emotion facing them. Alternatively, you could have the catcher act out an emotion, an activity specially suited for children.

The intent of this exercise is to discuss emotions with your family and practice listening to one another and expressing your feelings.

The Family Gift

This exercise can help a therapist to get to know a family better. If you are using it without the guidance of a therapist, it can help you to further your understanding of your own family and provoke thoughtful discussion.

To give this exercise a try, gather a variety of art supplies and a gift bag. Explain to the family that they are going to create a gift from the materials provided. This gift will be a gift for the whole family, that everyone in the family wants. They must decide together on this gift and how it can be used within their family.

They have 30 minutes to decide on this gift and craft it. Once they have created the gift, they must place it in the gift bag.

Within the context of family therapy, this exercise provides the therapist with a look at the inner workings of the family, how they make decisions and complete tasks as a unit.

If you are engaging in this exercise as a family without the presence of a therapist, it can help you to start a meaningful conversation.

Use these questions or prompts to facilitate the discussion:

1. Describe your gift.
2. Tell how you each felt as you were creating your gift.
3. Who made the decisions? For example, who decided what the gift should be?

4. Were two or more people in your family able to work well together?
5. Did anyone cause any difficulties or disagreements, and if so, how was this handled?
6. Is there anything about the way you did the activity that reminds you of how things work in your family at home?
7. How can the gift help your family? What else can help your family?

There is a wealth of information to be gained from observing these types of interactions or engaging in these kinds of discussion.

Genogram

A genogram is a schematic or graphic representation of a client's family tree. However, unlike the typical family tree, the genogram provides far more information on the relationships among members of the family.

It can be used to map out blood relations, medical conditions in the family, and, most often in the case of family therapy, emotional relationships.

Genograms contain two levels of information, that which is present on the traditional family tree and that which provides a much more comprehensive look at the family:

- Basic Information: name, gender, date of birth, date of death (if any).
- Additional Information: education, occupation, major life events, chronic illnesses, social behaviors, nature of family relationships, emotional relationships, social relationships, alcoholism, depression, diseases, alliances, and living situations.

By including this additional information, the therapist and client(s) can work together to identify patterns in the family history that may have influenced the client's current emotions and behaviors. Sometimes the simple act of mapping out and observing this information can make clear things which were previously unnoticed.

The information on emotional relationships can include points of interest and any aspects of the relationship that may have impacted the client(s), such as whether the relationship is marked by abuse, whether a marriage is separated or intact, if a relationship is characterized by love or indifference, whether a relationship could be considered "normal" or dysfunctional, etc.

This exercise could be completed individually, but it is likely to be most effective when completed in conjunction with a qualified professional.

How to create a Genogram

Genograms use a combination of special rules and symbols to depict a lot of information about families as succinctly as possible. Some of these rules and practices have been standardized, and should be followed so future readers can understand your documentation.

Other rules and symbols used in genograms differ depending on who you ask, or what reference you use. It isn't a big deal what symbols you use, as long as you are consistent. This will allow you to look at a genogram from any client—even those you don't know as well—and still glean useful information about their family.

Gender

Men are depicted by a square and women are depicted by a circle.

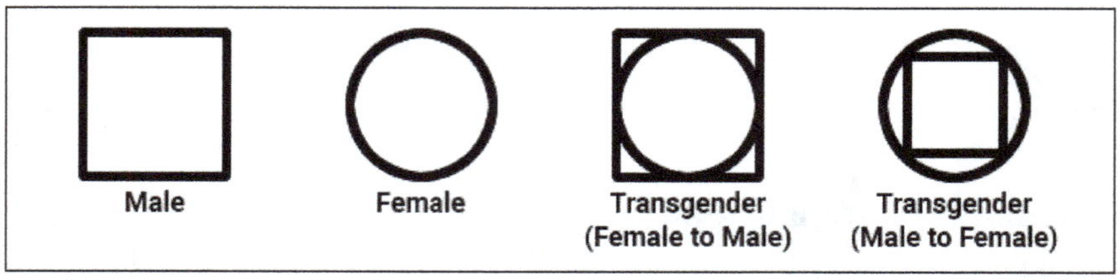

Family Relationships

Family relationships are depicted by two gender symbols connected by a line beneath them. Men should always appear on the left, and women on the right.

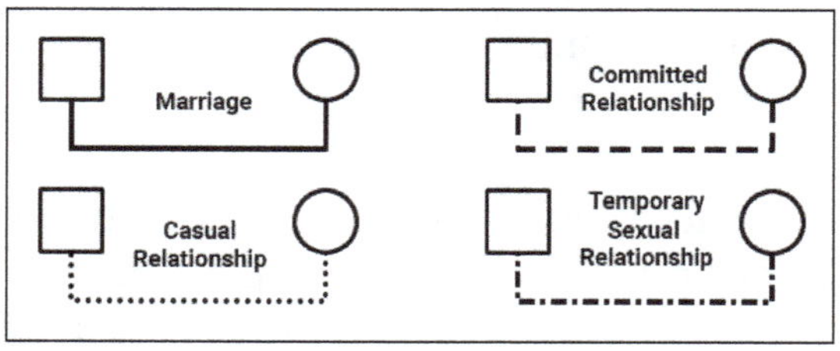

Descriptive symbols, which are placed on top of the family relationship line, give more detail about the relationship's status. Each of these symbols can be placed over any type of line (for example, the "separated" symbol could be placed over the "committed relationship" line or the "marriage" line).

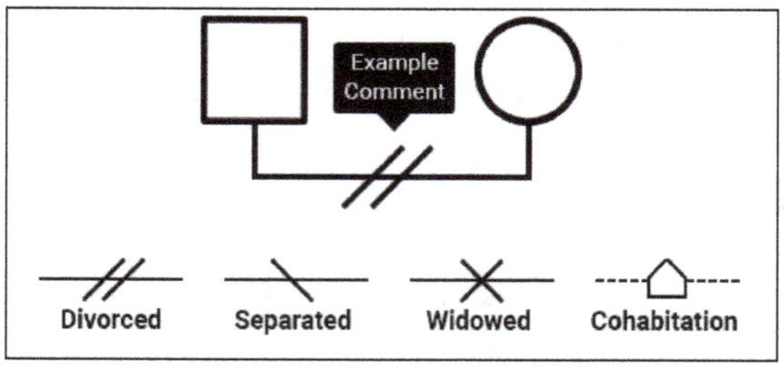

Emotional Relationships

Emotional relationships are depicted with a line directly connecting two gender symbols (different from family relationship connections, where the line is beneath them). These lines can be used to connect any two people on the genogram.

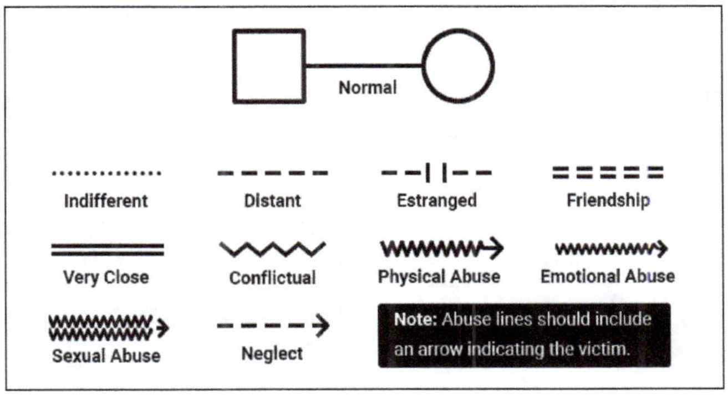

Your genograms will be very complicated if you connect every person to everyone else with emotional relationship lines. Try asking about each relationship, but only mark areas that are noteworthy or relevant to treatment.

Children

Children are placed beneath their parents, with a line stemming from the parents' family relationship line. Children should be listed from left to right, oldest to youngest.

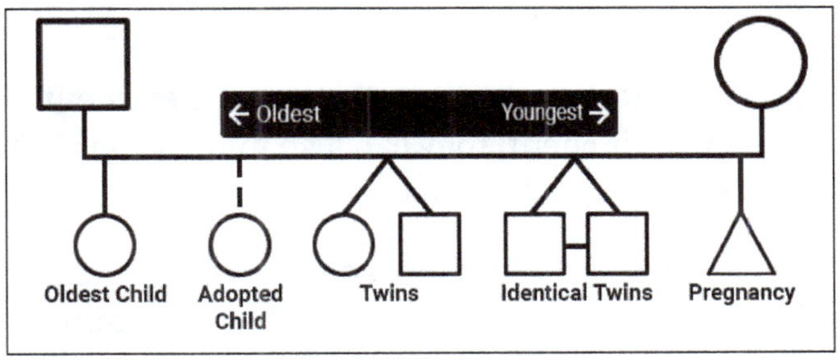

Lifespan

Deaths are indicated with an "X" inside the person's symbol. In some cases it may be important to add extra information such as a person's age, or dates related to birth and death.

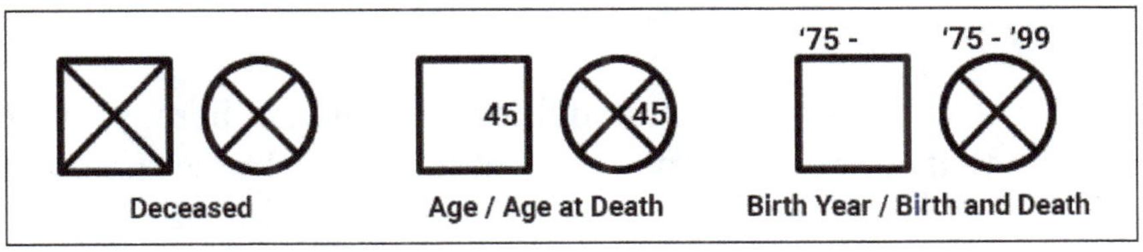

Additional Information

You can use genograms to depict just about anything that you think might be relevant to treatment. Feel free to create additional markers to fit your needs. For example, you might use an asterisk to indicate "difficulty with anger", or a squiggly line above a gender symbol to indicate "alcohol addiction".

Include a key whenever you use custom markers. Future you probably won't remember what the jumble of asterisks, squiggles, and diamonds mean.

Putting it All Together

Using the symbols and rules above, you should be able to construct a genogram that any other clinician can pick up and understand. Here's an example of completed genogram along with some commentary.

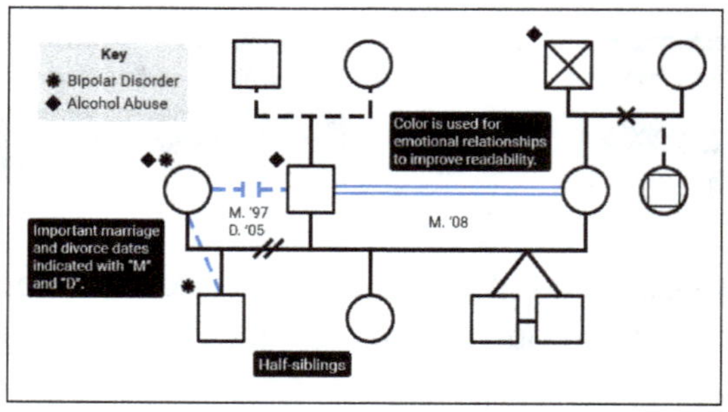

How to use Genograms in Psychotherapy

Assessment

Genograms fit in naturally during the assessment portion of treatment. Not only can genograms provide great information about your client, they can also inform you about family history of mental illness, which can give insight into possible diagnoses.

During family therapy, a genogram can also be used as a way to measure progress. Completing genograms at various points throughout treatment may help you and your clients see when and where there have been improvements to relationships.

Creating a genogram doesn't have to be a chore. Many people love to talk about their family, and will jump at the opportunity to share a few stories. This is a great opportunity to build rapport and get to know your client at the beginning of treatment.

Individual Therapy

All too often the importance of family is ignored during individual therapy, and genograms are a great way to make sure that your client's roots are not forgotten. In the same way that a person's ethnic or religious culture can shape their thoughts, feelings, and behaviors, so can their family culture. For this reason, clients struggling with a wide range of issues can benefit from learning about their family.

Family Therapy

The use of genograms in family therapy can be tricky because family members may see their relationships *very* differently from one another. However, these discrepancies can also be very telling. Consider the following example:

Example: A family consisting of two parents (Kori and Jason) and their daughter (Magnolia) come to your office for family therapy. While creating genograms, you notice that the parents both say Magnolia is distant, while Magnolia indicates that her parents are very close to one another, but distant from her.

In this example, it could be hypothesized that Magnolia and her parents both feel excluded from the other's world. Magnolia may feel that her parents care more about one another, yet the parents seem unaware of this. Kori and Jason might benefit from seeing that their daughter isn't just trying to be difficult. Instead, she might be afraid that her parents don't want her around.

Of course, these are just hypotheses. However, this example shows ways in which a genogram can act as a starting point for further exploration, and as a tool for initiating communication between family members.

Don't Forget Strengths

It's easy to get wrapped up in the negative traits that are passed down in families, so don't forget to spend some time on the strengths (especially during family therapy). If every session is spent railing on how dysfunctional a family is, why should they believe things can improve?

Sometimes, even the negative traits in a genogram can have a positive basis. Consider this example:

Example: Katy and her daughter Taylor both reveal through their genograms that they have an anger-fueled relationship with one another, as did Katy and her own mother. Now, Taylor is beginning to rebel.

After further exploration, Katy reveals that she rebelled against her own mother because she couldn't stand the constant lectures. However, Katy says she only lectures Taylor because she wants to help her avoid the same mistakes she made.

In this example, despite some noticeable issues with anger, we also see strengths. Katy is trying to help her daughter, although she seems to be going about it poorly. Her intentions come from a place of love. Focusing only on the anger would be likely to cause further division between Katy and Taylor.

Genograms are a great fit with many types of treatment, and many problem areas. Below, we've included a few references used for this guide.

Family Therapies

3

Depending on the conflict at hand, therapy may be targeted at analyzing previous instances of conflict or the sources of conflict through a better understanding of patterns of interaction. Therapists may also focus on the management and solution of problems rather than in the identification of a single cause. This chapter has been carefully written to provide an overview of family constellation therapy, strategic and structural family therapy, transgenerational family therapy, narrative therapy, etc.

Family Constellation Therapy

Family constellation is a type of therapy that's based on the idea that problems sift down through generations to cause stress in the here and now. Even if you don't know the traumas of your parents and earlier ancestors, you can learn them through the morphogenic field of energy that surrounds your family. By examining our feelings and perceptions in this 'field of knowing,' we can break out of familial patterns that cause us to suffer. We come to a resolution of these background issues through the family constellation, and our current problem can be easily solved.

Concepts In Family Constellations Therapy

Several concepts can add to your understanding of family constellation therapy.

Multigenerational Impact Of Trauma

Family constellations assume that anything that happened in your family line can affect the way you think, feel, and behave now. One person's grief, fear, or anger influences the entire family. Because family members are connected in the morphogenic field, they all feel effects of what has happened to each of the family members before them.

Morphogenic Field

The morphogenic field is an energy field that contains the memories and specific energies of a group. That group can be a family, a community, a country, or even the entire population of the world. Because this energy field contains all the knowledge from the group, experiencing its influence can help us understand the sources of our issues, even if no one has told us the facts.

Orders of Love

Bert Hellinger, the founder of family constellation therapy, identified several 'orders of love' from which love follows. The two most important and basic orders of love are that (1) everyone in the group has the same right to belong and always does belong, and (2) everyone who belongs must be given their specific rightful place.

Excluded Family Members

You might think, our family would never exclude one of our family members. It happens all the time. In family constellations, excluded family members are thought to affect the entire family, even after the family no longer has any contact with them. Some examples of excluded family members are:

- Babies who were miscarried or aborted.
- Babies or children who were given away for adoption.
- Family members who died, especially if they died young.
- Ex-spouses and partners from prior relationships.

These excluded family members continue to affect the whole family. Also, another family member may take their place, taking on their emotional struggles, addictions, or even their physical illnesses.

Drive to Belong

Family constellation therapy identifies the drive to belong as the greatest influencer in the family. If someone feels they don't belong, they'll do anything to get that feeling of belonging.

Hidden Loyalties

Within the family, we have loyalties. Sometimes, according to family constellations theory, we have loyalties to family members who died before us or who we never knew. These hidden loyalties can lead us to follow patterns, develop habits, and make unhealthy choices we can't understand with the factual information we have. Family constellation therapy can help us understand these sources so that we can make different decisions.

Uses for Family Constellations Therapy

Family constellation therapy can be used for a wide variety of problems, whether they're physical, mental, social, or spiritual issues. This therapy can help us overcome problems like:

- Depression
- Anxiety
- Addictions
- Bad habits
- Failure at work
- Negative relationship patterns
- Family dysfunction
- Trauma
- Grief
- Obsessive thoughts
- Physical illnesses
- Financial problems
- Phobias
- Excessive guilt

Family Constellation Therapy Methods

In a typical family constellation therapy session, there is a seeker, a facilitator, and possibly other participants. The seeker is the person who comes to resolve an issue. The facilitator is the therapist, who directs the constellation. The other participants are non related people who might also be seekers in their sessions.

The Seeker's Issue

The seeker has an issue they need to resolve or overcome. The issue can be anything from nail-biting or smoking to relationship issues or depression. They very briefly tell the facilitator what their issue is. They don't explain it in detail or suggests any reasons for why the issue exists and is troubling for them. Then, they sit down and observe.

Embodying the Family Constellation in A Group

If other people are involved in the session, the facilitator chooses different people to represent specific family members. The facilitator may also choose people to represent a group the seeker belongs to or an ideal they follow.

The facilitator then arranges the participants in a way that might be meaningful for the seeker. Everyone stays still for a time, giving the seeker time to connect with the morphogenic field and determine if the arrangement rings true for them.

Making Adjustments

The facilitator adjusts the arrangement until the seeker feels that it's 'right.' It takes some time to feel the truth or untruth of the arrangement each time. When the seeker accepts the arrangement, he or she will connect with it on the level of feelings and then, think.

At that point, the facilitator suggests a sentence for each of the participants to say. The seeker takes their place in the family constellation, and each person says their sentence. Again, if the suggestion doesn't ring true for them, the facilitator can try again.

Resolving Emotional Distresses

After the family constellation exercise is over, the seeker, having learned the source of their current issue, goes back to their life to learn more about that person or part of their past. If that person is still alive, the can connect with them directly on an emotional level to bring healing to the relationship. If the person is deceased or otherwise unavailable, the seeker looks for other ways to learn about what happened in the past so that they can find their resolutions to those lingering ancestral issues.

Family Constellation Therapy Settings

Family constellation therapy typically takes place either in a workshop or individual counseling sessions. Both ways have proven effective, although different methods are needed for each.

Workshops

In family constellation workshops, people take turns being the seeker and the participants. The procedure is much like the one explained above.

Individual Counseling

In individual counseling, family constellation therapy often takes the form of imaginative solo exercises. The therapist may suggest you imagine a situation in which you connect with an excluded family member or you, if you're the excluded family member, connect with a member of members of the family. In this way, you resolve the source of your problem. The idea is that once this source is healed, your current problem will disappear.

Strategic and Structural Family Therapy

Strategic and Structural family therapy has been heavily influenced by Bateson's cybernetics model. They are mostly intent upon changing behavior rather than insight, and as such are famous for creative interventions. There are 3 main models in this theory:

A. The Mental Research Institute (MRI) - Started by Jackson who worked with Bateson, as well as with Haley on the Bateson project.

B. The Haley and Madanes Strategic approach- They were heavily influenced by Erikson, Bateson, and Minuchin. Erikson believed the unconscious was full of wisdom - thus, he didn't need to give people insight, just help them get access to it on their own.

C. The Milan Model - Palazzoli was a prominent Italian psychoanalyst. She and her team of 8 other analysts read the works of Bateson, Haley and did lots of research. In 1980, they split, with ½ continuing research and the other doing training.

Major Assumptions

A. MRI - families make common-sense but misguided attempts to solve their problems. The solution selection as well as its success is governed by system rules. The attempts go awry and the result is a positive feedback loop that makes the problem worse. What do you do?

a. Identify the feedback loop

b. Find the rules governing it

c. Change the loops and rules.

They are not interested in long term change, insight, or what function the symptom serves in the family; only problem focused behavioral change is important.

B. Haley and Madanes followed these same Ideas, but with some Variations

1. Haley and Madanes were concerned with the function a symptom served, as it marked a payoff in the system that resulted due to the structure of the system. Haley and Madanes studied triadic interaction over long periods of time, say months. Haley even wrote a book on Leaving Home. Haley was particularly concerned with power struggles, and often prescribed the symptom such that the cost of keeping it up outweighed the gains. Madanes was concerned with incongruous hierarchies, where a child uses symptoms to change the behavior of the parent.

2. Haley and Madanes also formulated that rules followed a hierarchical order, and thus improving the hierarchical and boundary problems would prevent dysfunctional feedback loops from starting, a sort of "plan ahead" strategy.

3. Haley and Madanes believe families go through dysfunctional stages to get to functional ones.

4. Finally, Madanes posits four categories of problems resulting from;

   a. desire to control and dominate

   b. desire to be loved

   c. desire to love and protect others

   d. desire to repent and forgive

Thus, Haley and Madanes are interested more in short sequences, but also in long ones that last months or years and reflect chronic structural problems.

C. The Milan Group read and followed many of the works of MRI and Haley and Madanes, worked with power struggles and boundaries as well, and focused on long time spans spanning even multiple generations. They worked mostly with anorexic and schizophrenic families.

Theoretical Formulations

A. Normal Family Development

1. The MRI group disdains concepts of "normality." They do, however, believe that families should be able to shift solutions when they aren't working, in order to prevent a run away positive feedback loop

2. Haley and Madanes emphasized clear generational boundaries, like the Milan group, but did hold a concept of normality and believed therapy should change the dysfunctional structure and create a more functional one.

3. The Milan group, like the MRI, also disdains concepts of "normality." They do, like Haley and Madanes, believe that families should have clear generational boundaries. However, unlike Haley and Madanes but like the MRI's, they believe that the therapy should be "neutral" and not have expectations of families. This way, the therapy helps the family by simply examining the family, asking questions to help them examine their own family structure, and exposing games after which they can redesign their family into a better structure on their own.

B. Problematic Family Development

There are three models for problem development;

a. Cybernetic (runaway positive feedback loops)

b. Structural (flawed family hierarchies)

c. Functional (one member develops symptoms to control others).

The MRI use only the cybernetic model, Haley and Madanes use all 3 but Haley stresses the structural and Madanes the functional, and the Milan's use both structural and functional.

Example

Tommy is 16 and has recently refused to go out of the house.

1. MRI would focus on getting Tommy out, believing the parents attempted solutions kept him home.

2. Haley and Madanes would focus on the triadic relationship between Tommy and his 2 parents. Haley would wonder about the parents unresolved conflicts and marital struggles, Madanes would wonder about how Tommy staying home helped one or both of his parents.

3. Milan would focus on the family's history and hidden power struggles, or family games, in which Tommy is embedded and has to stay home to help a family member "win."

C. Goals for Therapy

1. MRI simply change the current problem (run away positive feedback loop) and send the family home, even if there are other serious problems. Unless the family asks for help on other problems, the therapy doesn't intervene. MRI's help the family by making them form clear, straight forward, immediate, behavioral goals and sticking to them.

2. Haley is also behavioral, concerned with the immediate problem, and anti- insight. Unlike MRI, he wanted a structural re-organization of the family, like the structural therapies, but

one which would proceed in steps and have sub-goals along the way all dealing with the presenting problem.

While strategic therapy don't use relationships and personality (supposedly) to achieve their goals and instead rely on strategies, by focusing on the problem at hand, he kept resistance down and built trust with the family. After the immediate problem is resolved, Haley would explore other problems (unlike MRI), but only at this point after building trust. Therapy did not necessarily end with the immediate problem resolves, but could end with the change in the structural factors that caused the problem.

While both Haley and Madanes take responsibility for change, Madanes believes that additional goals such as happiness and the ability to work, love, and play are important also.

3. Milan held that the therapy was responsible for change, and had to basically manipulate and outwit the family and their games though strategies designed to expose games and reframe member's motives. Palazzoli focused on exposing "dirty games," and Boscolo on understanding the games and the family better. Boscolo did not take responsibility for the family's change, and wanted to collude with them and get them to make their own changes to whatever new structure they would devise.

D.Conditions for Change

1. MRI believed that by attempting first order change, or change in the behavior, second order change, or change in the system's structure, could be achieved. They don't need insight as to why they have problems, nor do they need to understand why the change in behavior is needed. They simply need to act differently and see for themselves that the family's rules for problem-solving can be more flexible. They try to keep resistance low and motivation high.
2. Haley and Madanes also believed insight to be of little use, tried to keep resistance low, and focused on behavioral change, arguing that before the family can think or feel differently, they must act differently.
3. The Milan also try to keep resistance low and motivation high. They also try to find the "customer" or the most motivated family member and work with them. While they may not have the "problem," they may be the most motivated for change, and since one person can change a system, they may be the most successful level to use in producing change.

How to do Strategic and Structural Family Therapy

The Strategic approach focused mostly on strategies adapted to the specific situation of the person and problem, as did Erikson. Each of the three models is somewhat different.

A. MRI Techniques - there are basically 6 steps to treatment

1. Introduction and setup - MRI's limit session to 10 and set up a powerful motivator
2. Definition of the problem in clear behavioral terms
3. Estimation of the behavior (run away positive feedback loops) maintaining the problem
4. Setting goals
5. Selecting and making interventions
    a. Reframing - providing the family with a rational for treatment. The MRI therapist may not believe what they tell the family, but that is unimportant as long as its a rational explanation. The point of it is not to bring insight, but to induce compliance.
    b. Outpositioning - having someone take the role other family members place on them to the extreme.
    c. Paradoxical interventions - compliance based, to simply get the family to change their behavior by complying with a directive, or defiance based, in the hopes that the family will defy the directive and improve.
    d. Symptom prescription or an exposure based paradox - to expose the family's hidden relationships.
    e. Restraining techniques - telling the family they can't move very fast because they aren't ready.
6. Termination.

B. Haley and Madanes use many of the same strategies listed above, but with the hope of changing the family's structure in the long run. Therapy begins by:

1. A social stage - everyone is greeted and spoken to in order to make everyone feel more relaxed and less defensive.
2. A problem stage - introduce yourself and repeat what you know, then speak to each person and get their opinions and ideas about the problem. Haley engages the father first, and observes all the family members interactions to uncover hidden triangles.
3. An interaction stage - Haley has members talk about differing perspectives on the problem. He can observe then the family interactions around the problem. By asking what they have tried before, he gains information and also underscores the family's need of his help. Haley may end a first session with a simple directive, not advice, but a directive. Haley may prescribe some ordeal, such that the cost of maintaining the symptom is more than the benefit of the symptom. Usually each member is told they will benefit from the directive to increase compliance. Madanes often had people follow a directive by telling them it was just for pretend or play. Haley focused more on restoring power to the parents, while Madanes focused more on creating new and pleasurable interactions for the parent

and child. Madanes developed a classification system for families, as well as guidelines for when to use hers, Haley's, or MRI techniques.

C. Milan - There are several Milan models. The original model was very strategic. Families were treated by a male and female cotherapist team; therapy were observed by other members of the team; families were seen once a month for only 10 sessions. Therapy were supposed to be neutral and distant. Sessions had 5 parts

1. Presession - tentative hypothesis are made
2. Session - the hypothesis are tested and refined
3. Intersession - the team would meet with the therapy while the family waited
4. Intervention - the therapy would return to deliver the intervention. There are several interventions usually used
    a. Positive connotation - reframe the problem but in a way that the family members are not blamed or labeled as bad.
    b. Rituals were directives to engage the whole family in some behavior that exaggerated or broke rules and family myths. Family members may thank each other for their respective symptoms, mother and father may alternate days for parental responsibilities.
5. Post-session - the team would analyze the family's reaction and plan for the next session.

Transgenerational Family Therapy

Transgenerational theories of family therapy are typically associated with the works of Murray Bowen, Ivan Boszormenyi-Nagy, James Framo, and Don Williamson. Family therapy texts include these approaches among the major family therapy theories. These theorists use the terms transgenerational, intergenerational, and multigenerational as well as family systems theory to classify their theories, each term having its own particular connotation. While we claim no prejudice, for the purposes of this paper, the term transgenerational is used. Family therapy texts are often unclear as to the methods for translating transgenerational theory into practice. Behavioral skills are not always evident or easily inferred from the abstract concepts of the theories.

Transgenerational models of family therapy are similar in that they (a) value historical information, (b) believe in the influence of the past on the present (and the future), and (c) strive to accomplish more than simple symptom reduction. These approaches are systemic in that they conceptualize emotional pain as arising out of interactional, human systems, primarily families of origin. Psychic dynamics dwell within the context of interactions, relationships, and myths (value and belief systems). These models focus on family-of-origin and transgenerational dynamics as the unit of analysis. The models differ in the particular language used (e.g., loyalties, personal authority, or differentiation) and the particular clients seen in therapy (an individual, a family, or subsets of a family). But how do the transgenerational family therapy approaches translate to actual training? More specifically, what are the basic, fundamental skills or competencies of those who practice this approach?

Transgenerational Family Therapy Skills

According to the Manual on Accreditation (Commission on Accreditation for Marriage and Family Therapy Education, students in AAMFT accredited programs are expected to begin seeing clients early in their programs. For many students, particularly those with no prior counseling experience, this can be a highly stressful situation. From the perspective of Bowen's theory, the ensuing anxiety and emotional intensity can inhibit thinking and thus diminish therapy for both the clients and the therapist. Bowen stresses that intervention emanates primarily from the differentiated, calm therapist rather than from technique. This requires a focus on the self of the therapist as a crucial component of training. Students attracted to the concepts of transgenerational therapy do not always wish to wait for their self-work to be complete before using the ideas with clients; simultaneous self-work and therapy training could enhance both processes. Therefore, an understanding of some of the basic skills and competencies of transgenerational family therapy, empirically derived, could be used to guide the training and self-exploration of beginning family therapists. The skills could also serve as valuable markers when assessing trainees for their readiness to advance as therapists or as evidence that they need more training or selfwork. In addition, if research is to uncover some of the truths of transgenerational therapy, abstract as they are, we must have operational definitions of the skills used in therapy. Identification of the skills associated with transgenerational therapy will assist in both outcome and process research.

Narrative Therapy

Narrative therapy is a form of psychotherapy that seeks to help people identify their values and the skills and knowledge they have to live these values, so they can effectively confront whatever problems they face. The therapist seeks to help the person co-author a new narrative about themselves by investigating the history of those qualities. Narrative therapy claims to be a social justice approach to therapeutic conversations, seeking to challenge dominant discourses that it claims shape people's lives in destructive ways. The approach was developed during the 1970s and 1980s, largely by Australian social worker Michael White and David Epston of New Zealand.

While narrative work is typically located within the field of family therapy, many authors and practitioners report using these ideas and practices in community work, schools and higher education.

Identity

The narrative therapist focuses upon assisting people to create stories about themselves, about their identities, that are helpful to them. This work of "re-authoring identity" claims to help people identify their own values and identify the skills and knowledge they have to live these values. Through the process of identifying the history of values in people's lives, the therapist is able to co-author a new story about the person.

Michael White

The story people tell about themselves and that is told about them is important in this approach which asserts that the story of person's identity determines what they think is possible for themselves. The narrative process allows people to identify what values are important to them and how they might use their own skills and knowledge to live these values.

Externalizing the Problem

The concept of identity is important in narrative therapy. The approach aims not to conflate people's identities with the problems they may face or the mistakes they have made. Rather, the approach seeks to avoid modernist, essentialist notions of the self that lead people to believe there is a biologically determined "true self" or "true nature". Instead, identity, seen as primarily social, can be changed according to the choices people make.

To separate people's identities from the problems they face, narrative therapy employs externalizing conversations. The process of externalization allows people to consider their relationships with problems; thus the narrative motto: "The person is not the problem, the problem is the problem." So-called strengths or positive attributes also are externalized, allowing people to engage in the construction and performance of preferred identities.

Therapeutic Posture

In a narrative approach, the therapist aims to adopt a collaborative therapeutic posture rather than imposing ideas on people by giving them advice. Both the therapist and the people who consult them are seen as having valuable information both in terms of the process of therapeutic conversation and in terms of the content of these conversations. By adopting a posture of curiosity and collaboration instead, the therapist aims to give the implicit message to people that they have already knowledge and skills to solve the problems they face. When people develop solutions to their own problems on the basis of their own values, they become much more committed to implementing these solutions.

Common Elements

Common elements in narrative therapy are:

- The assumption that narratives or stories shape a person's identity, as when a person assesses a problem in their life for its effects and influences as a "dominant story";
- An appreciation for the creation and use of documents, as when a person and a counselor co-author "A Graduation from the Blues Certificate";
- An "externalizing" emphasis, such as by naming a problem so that a person can assess its effects in his or her life, come to know how it operates or works in their life, relate their earliest history, evaluate it to take a definite position on its presence, and in the end choose their relationship to it.
- A focus on "unique outcomes" (a term of Erving Goffman) or exceptions to the problem that wouldn't be predicted by the problem's narrative or story itself.
- A strong awareness of the impact of power relations in therapeutic conversations, with a commitment to checking back with the client about the effects of therapeutic styles in order to mitigate the possible negative effect of invisible assumptions or beliefs held by the therapist.
- Responding to personal failure conversations.

Outsider Witnesses

In this particular narrative practice or conversation, outsider witnesses are invited listeners to a consultation. Often they are friends of the consulting person or past clients of the therapist who have their own knowledge and experience of the problem at hand. During the first interview, between therapist and consulting person, the outsider listens without comment.

Then the therapist interviews them with the instructions not to critique or evaluate or make a proclamation about what they have just heard, but instead to simply say what phrase or image stood out for them, followed by any resonances between their life struggles and those just witnessed. Lastly, the outsider is asked in what ways they may feel a shift in how they experience themselves from when they first entered the room.

Next, in similar fashion, the therapist turns to the consulting person, who has been listening all the while, and interviews them about what images or phrases stood out in the conversation just heard and what resonances have struck a chord within them.

In the end, an outsider witness conversation is often rewarding for witnesses. But for the consulting person the outcomes are remarkable: they learn they are not the only one with this problem, and they acquire new images and knowledge about it and their chosen alternate direction in life. The main aim of the narrative therapy is to engage in people's problems by providing the alternative best solution.

Criticisms

To date, there have been several formal criticisms of narrative therapy over what are viewed as its theoretical and methodological inconsistencies, among various other concerns.

- Stories empower people to self-prescribe narrative therapy. Not only do people know which story they like, but they also know which narrative they need to escape from reality as well as transform it.
- Narrative therapy has been criticised as holding to a social constructionist belief that there are no absolute truths, but only socially sanctioned points of view, and that Narrative therapists therefore privilege their client's concerns over and above "dominating" cultural narratives.
- Several critics have posed concerns that narrative therapy has made gurus of its leaders, particularly in the light that its leading proponents tend to be overly harsh about most other kinds of therapy. Others have criticized narrative therapy for failing to acknowledge that the individual Narrative therapist may bring personal opinions and biases into the therapy session.
- Narrative therapy is also criticized for the lack of clinical and empirical studies to validate its many claims. Etchison & Kleist state that narrative therapy's focus on qualitative outcomes is not congruent with larger quantitative research and findings which the majority of respected empirical studies employ today. This has led to a lack of research material which can support its claims of efficacy.

How to use Various Narrative Therapy Techniques

Telling One's Story (Putting Together a Narrative)

As a therapist or other mental health professional, your job in narrative therapy is to help your client find their voice and tell their story in their own words. According to the philosophy behind narrative therapy, storytelling is how we make meaning and find purpose in our own experience.

Helping your client develop their story gives them an opportunity to discover meaning, find healing, and establish or re-establish an identity, all integral factors for success in therapy.

This technique is also known as "re-authoring" or "re-storying," as clients explore their own experiences to find alterations to their story or make a whole new one. The same events can tell a hundred different stories since we all interpret experiences differently and find different senses of meaning (Dulwich Centre).

Externalization Technique

The externalization technique involves leading your client toward viewing their problems or behaviors as external, instead of a part of him or her. This is a technique that is much easier to describe than to fully embrace, but it can have huge positive impacts on self-identity and confidence.

The general idea of this technique is that it is much easier to change a behavior that you engage in than it is to change a characteristic that is a part of you. For example, if you are quick to anger and you consider yourself an angry person, you must fundamentally change something about yourself to address the problem; however, if you are a person who acts aggressively and becomes angry easily, you simply need to alter the behaviors to address the problem.

It might seem like an insignificant distinction, but there is a profound difference between the mindset of someone who labels themselves as a "problem" person and someone who acknowledges they sometimes engage in problematic behavior.

As a therapist, this technique is easy to describe, but it may be challenging for the client to fully buy into this strange idea. Encourage your client not to place too much importance on their diagnosis or self-assigned labels. Let them know how empowering it can be to separate him- or herself from their problems, allowing them a greater degree of control.

Deconstruction Technique

This "deconstruction" refers to breaking down the problem or problems the client is having, making it more easy to understand and address. Our problems can often feel overwhelming, confusing, or unsolvable, but they are never truly unsolvable.

Deconstructing the issue makes it more specific and avoids overgeneralizing, as well as clarifying what the core issue or issues actually are.

As an example of the deconstruction technique, imagine two people in a long-term relationship who are having trouble. One partner is feeling frustrated with a partner who never shares her feelings, thoughts, or ideas with him.

Based on this short description, there is no clear idea of what the problem is, let alone what the solution might be. If you, as a therapist, were to deconstruct the problem with this client, you might ask him to be more specific about what is bothering him.

This might lead to a better idea of what is troubling the man, like feeling lonely and missing a sense of intimacy with his partner. From here, you might find that intimacy is very important for this man in romantic relationships, and when his partner doesn't share with him he is left feeling isolated and like his partner doesn't truly trust him.

Deconstructing the problem helped us to learn exactly what the problem is (he is feeling lonely and isolated) and what this means to him (it makes him feel like his partner doesn't trust him, or perhaps is not willing to commit to the relationship like he is).

This technique is an excellent way to help the client dig deep into the problem, understanding what is important to them and how this issue threatens that.

Unique Outcomes Technique

This technique is a bit involved and complex, but keep in mind the storytelling aspect of narrative therapy.

The unique outcomes technique involves changing one's own storyline. In narrative therapy, the client aims to construct a storyline to their experiences which provides meaning and gives them a positive, functional identity. We are not limited to just one storyline, though. There are many potential storylines we can subscribe to, some more negative and others more positive.

Instead of continuing to see his or her life from the same perspective as always, the unique outcomes technique can help a client to change their perspective and perceive more positive and life-giving narratives.

Like a book that switches viewpoints from one character to another, our life has multiple threads of narrative running through it with different perspectives, different areas of focus, and different points of interest. Putting the unique outcomes technique to use is simply choosing to focus on a different storyline or storylines from the one that has been the source of your problems.

Using this technique might sound like avoiding the problem, but it's actually just reimagining the problem. What seems like a problem or issue from one perspective can be nothing but an unassuming or insignificant detail in another.

As a therapist, you can introduce this technique by encouraging your client(s) to pursue alternative or new storylines.

Existentialism

You might have a particular association with the term "existentialism" that makes its presence here seem odd, but there is likely more to existentialism than you think.

Existentialism is not a bleak and hopeless view on a world without meaning.

It's true that, in general, existentialists believe the world holds no inherent meaning, but they do not take this belief as a license to fall into a deep pit of depression and meaninglessness; rather, they believe we can create our own meaning.

In this way, existentialism and narrative therapy go hand in hand. Narrative therapy encourages individuals to make their own meaning and find their own purpose rather than search for some pre-existing, absolute truth.

Borrowing some techniques or interventions from existentialism can provide excellent support for the client working through narrative therapy.

If your client is an avid reader, you might consider suggesting some existentialist works as well, such as those by Jean-Paul Sartre, Albert Camus, or Martin Heidegger.

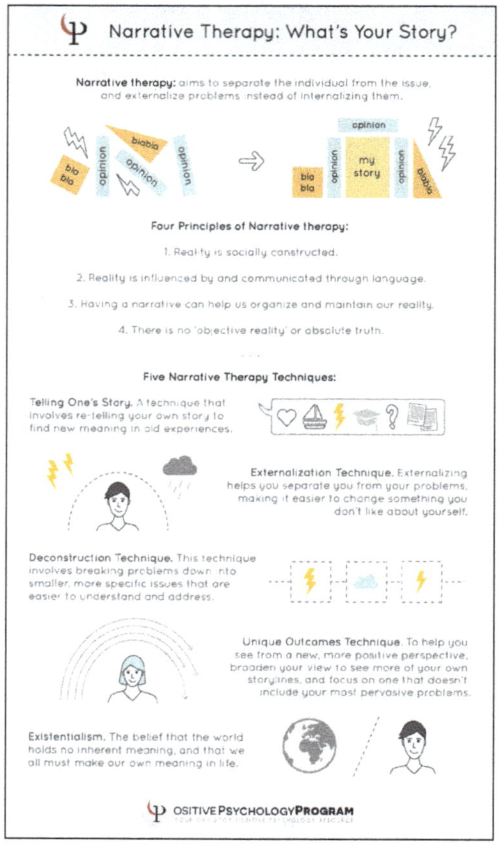

3 More Narrative Therapy Exercises and Interventions

While narrative therapy is more of a dialogue between the therapist and client, there are some exercises and activities to supplement the regular therapy sessions. A few of these are described below.

Statement of Position Map

This simple handout consists of four areas to be filled in:

1. Characteristics and naming or labeling of the problem
2. Mapping the effects of the problem throughout each domain of life it touches (home, work, school, relationships, etc.)
3. Evaluation of the effects of the problem in these domains
4. Values that come up when thinking about why these effects are undesirable.

This map is intended to be filled out in concert with a therapist, but it could be explored individually if it is difficult to find or meet with a narrative therapist.

Generally, the dialogue between a therapist and client will delve into these four areas. The therapist will ask questions and probe for deeper inquiry, while the client talks through the problem they are having and finds insight into each of the four main areas listed above.

There is power in the simple act of naming the problem, and it is necessary to understand how and in which areas the problem is having an effect. Finally, it is vital for the client to understand why this problem bothers them on a deeper level. What values are being infringed upon or obstructed by this problem? Why does the client feel negative about the problem? These are questions that this exercise can help to answer.

My Life Story

One of the most basic therapeutic principles in narrative therapy is that we find meaning and healing through telling stories. This exercise is all about your story, and all you need is the printout and a pen or pencil.

The intention of the My Life Story exercise is to separate yourself from your past to gain a broader perspective on your life. It aims to help you create an outline of your life without diving too deeply into your memories.

First, you write the title of the book that is your life. Maybe it is simply "Monica's Life Story," or something more reflective of the themes you see in your life, like "Monica: A Story of Perseverance."

In the next section, come up with at least seven chapter titles, each one representing a significant stage or event in your life. Once you have the chapter title, come up with one sentence that sums up the chapter. For example, your chapter title could be "Awkward and Uncertain" and the description may read "My teenage years were dominated by a sense of uncertainty and confusion in a family of seven."

Next, you will consider your final chapter and add a description of your life in the future. What will you do in the future? Where will you go, and who will you be? This is where you get to flex your predictive muscles.

Finally, the last step is to add to your chapters as necessary to put together a comprehensive story of your life.

This exercise will help you to organize your thoughts and beliefs about your life and weave together a story that makes sense to you. The idea is not to get too deep into any specific memories but to recognize that what is in your past is truly the past. It shaped you, but it does not have to define you.

Expressive Arts

This intervention can be especially useful for children, but many adults may find relief and meaning through engagement as well.

We all have different methods of telling our stories, and using the arts to do so has been a staple of humanity for countless generations.

To take advantage of this expressive and creative way to tell your stories, explore the different methods at your disposal. You can:

- *Meditate.* Guided relaxation or individual meditation can be an extremely effective way to explore a problem.
- *Journal.* Journaling has many potential benefits, and this is yet another. You can consider a specific set of question s (e.g., How does the problem affect you? How did the problem take hold in your life?) or simply write a description of yourself or your story from the point of view of the problem. This can be difficult but can lead to a greater understanding of the problem and how it influences the domains of your life.
- *Draw.* If you're more interested in depictions of the problem's impact on your experience, you can use your skills to draw or paint the effects of the problem. You can create a symbolic drawing, map the effects of the problem, or create a cartoon that represents the problem in your life.
- *Movement.* You can use the simple medium of movement and mindfulness to create and express your story. Begin by moving in your usual way, then allow the problem to influence your movement. Practice mindful observation to see what changes when you let the problem take hold. Next, develop a transitional movement that begins to shake the problem's hold on you. Finally, transition into a "liberation movement" to metaphorically and physically explore how to escape the problem.

- Visualization. Use visualization techniques to consider how your life might turn out in a week, a month, a year, or a few years, both with this problem continuing and in a timeline in which you embrace a new direction. Share your experience with a partner or therapist, or reflect on your experience in your journal to explore the ways in which this exercise helped you find meaning or new possibilities for your life.

Examples of Questions to Ask your Clients

"Every time we ask a question, we're generating a possible version of a life." – David Epston

Narrative therapy is a dialogue in which both you and your client converse to learn about your story. As you may imagine, it requires many questions on the part of the therapist.

The list of questions below is intended to go with the statement of position maps, but these questions can be extremely useful outside of this exercise as well:

- It sounds as though [problem] is part of your life now.
- How long have you been noticing this [problem]?
- What effect does the [problem] have on your life?
- How does the [problem] impact on your energy for daily tasks?
- Does [problem] have an impact on your relationship with other family members?
- What effects does [problem] have on your child's life?
- What do you think about the effects [problem] is having on your life?
- Are you accepting what [problem] is doing?
- Are these effects acceptable to you or not?
- Why is this? Why are you taking this position on what [problem] is doing?
- How would you prefer things to be?
- If you were to stay connected to what you have just said about what you prefer, what next steps could you take?

Some excellent examples of questions you can ask your client as you move through their story:

Enabling Openings

Can you describe the last time you managed to get free of the problem for a couple of minutes? What was the first thing you noticed in those few minutes? What was the next thing?

Linking Openings with Preferred Experience

Would you like more minutes like these in your life?

Moving from Openings to Alternative Story Development

What was each of you thinking/feeling/doing/wishing/imagining during those few minutes?

Broadening the Viewpoint

What might your friend have noticed about you if she had met up with you in those few minutes?

Exploring Landscapes of Action

How did you achieve that? How did Tim help you with that?

Exploring Landscapes of Consciousness

What have you learned about what you can manage from those few minutes?

Linking with the Exceptions in the Past

Tell me about times when you have managed to achieve a similar few minutes in the past?

Linking Exceptions from the Past with the Present

When you think about those times in the past when you have achieved this, how might this alter your view of the problem now?

Linking Exceptions from the Past with the Future

Thinking about this now, what do you expect to do next?

Narrative Therapy Treatment Plan

Coming up with a treatment plan for narrative therapy is a personal and intensive activity to be completed within the therapeutic relationship, but there are some guidelines on how to set up an effective plan.

(1) Externalization of the problem, which mirrors the steps of the statement of position mapping exercise:

Developing a particular, experience-near definition of the problem

Mapping the effects of the problem

Evaluating the effects of the problem

Justifying the evaluation

(2) Re-authoring conversations, or helping the client include neglected aspects of themselves that do not fit within the problem-centered narrative.

(3) Remembering conversations, which focuses on actively engaging the client in the process of renewing their relationships, removing the relationships they no longer want, and finding meaning in aspects of their story not prevalent in the negative, problem-saturated story.

Marriage Counseling

4

Marriage counseling or marriage therapy is aimed at improving romantic relationships and resolving interpersonal conflicts. The topics elucidated in this chapter address some of the techniques of couples counseling for conflict resolution, premarital counseling, divorce therapy, family planning counseling, etc.

Couple's therapy (also couples' counseling or marriage therapy) attempts to improve romantic relationships and resolve interpersonal conflicts.

Basic Principles

Before a relationship between individuals can begin to be understood, it is important to recognize and acknowledge that each person, including the counselor, has a unique personality, perception, set of values and history. Individuals in the relationship may adhere to different and unexamined value systems. Institutional and societal variables (like the social, religious, group and other collective factors) which shape a person's nature and behavior are considered in the process of counseling and therapy. A tenet of relationship counseling is that it is intrinsically beneficial for all the participants to interact with each other and with society at large with optimal amounts of conflict. A couple's conflict resolution skills seems to predict divorce rates.

Most relationships will get strained at some time, resulting in a failure to function optimally and produce self-reinforcing, maladaptive patterns. These patterns may be called "negative interaction cycles." There are many possible reasons for this, including insecure attachment, ego, arrogance, jealousy, anger, greed, poor communication/understanding or problem solving, ill health, third parties and so on.

Changes in situations like financial state, physical health, and the influence of other family members can have a profound influence on the conduct, responses and actions of the individuals in a relationship.

Often it is an interaction between two or more factors, and frequently it is not just one of the people who are involved that exhibit such traits. Relationship influences are reciprocal: it takes each person involved to make and manage problems.

A viable solution to the problem and setting these relationships back on track may be to reorient the individuals' perceptions and emotions - how one looks at or responds to situations and feels about them. Perceptions of and emotional responses to a relationship are contained within an often unexamined mental map of the relationship, also called a love map by John Gottman. These can be explored collaboratively and discussed openly. The core values they comprise can then be understood and respected or changed when no longer appropriate. This implies that each person takes equal responsibility for awareness of the problem as it arises, awareness of their own contribution to the problem and making some fundamental changes in thought and feeling.

The next step is to adopt conscious, structural changes to the inter-personal relationships and evaluate the effectiveness of those changes over time.

Indeed, "typically for those close personal relations there is a certain degree in 'interdependence' - which means that the partners are alternately mutually dependent on each other. As a special aspect of such relations something contradictory is put outside: the need for intimacy and for autonomy."

"The common counterbalancing satisfaction these both needs, intimacy and autonomy, leads to alternately satisfaction in the relationship and stability. But it depends on the specific developing duties of each partner in every life phase and maturity".

Basic Practices

Two methods of couples therapy focus primarily on the process of communicating. The most commonly used method is active listening, used by the late Carl Rogers and Virginia Satir, and recommended by Harville Hendrix in *Getting the Love You Want*. More recently, a method called "Cinematic Immersion" has been developed by Warren Farrell in *Women Can't Hear What Men Don't Say*. Each helps couples learn a method of communicating designed to create a safe environment for each partner to express and hear feelings.

When the Munich Marital Study discovered active listening to not be used in the long run, Warren Farrell observed that active listening did a better job creating a safe environment for the criticizer to criticize than for the listener to hear the criticism. The listener, often feeling overwhelmed by the criticism, tended to avoid future encounters. He hypothesized that we were biologically programmed to respond defensively to criticism, and therefore the listener needed to be trained in-depth with mental exercises and methods to interpret as love what might otherwise feel abusive. His method is Cinematic Immersion.

After 30 years of research into marriage John Gottman has found that healthy couples almost never listen and echo each other's feelings naturally. Whether miserable or radiantly happy, couples said what they thought about an issue, and "they got angry or sad, but their partner's response was never anything like what we were training people to do in the listener/speaker exercise, not even close."

Such exchanges occurred in less than 5 percent of marital interactions and they predicted nothing about whether the marriage would do well or badly. What's more, Gottman noted, data from a 1984 Munich study demonstrated that the (reflective listening) exercise itself didn't help couples to improve their marriages. To teach such interactions, whether as a daily tool for couples or as a therapeutic exercise in empathy, was a clinical dead end.

> By contrast emotionally focused therapy for couples (EFT-C) is based on attachment theory and uses emotion as the target and agent of change. Emotions bring the past alive in rigid interaction patterns, which create and reflect absorbing emotional states. As one of its founders Sue Johnson says,

Forget about learning how to argue better, analysing your early childhood, making grand romantic gestures, or experimenting with new sexual positions. Instead, recognize and admit that you are emotionally attached to and dependent on your partner in much the same way that a child is on a parent for nurturing, soothing, and protection.

Research on Therapy

The most researched approach to couples therapy is behavioral couples therapy. It is a well established treatment for marital discord. This form of therapy has evolved to what is now called integrative behavioral couples therapy. Integrative behavioral couples therapy appears to be effective for 69% of couples in treatment, while the traditional model was effective for 50-60% of couples. At five-year follow-up, the marital happiness of the 134 couples who had participated in either integrative behavioral couples therapy or traditional couples therapy showed that 14% of relationships remained unchanged, 38% deteriorated, and 48% improved or recovered completely.

How to Become a Marriage Counselor

Step 1: Obtain a Bachelor's Degree

Earning a bachelor's degree is typically required prior to enrolling in a master's degree program, which is required for marriage counselors. Most schools do not offer bachelor's degree programs specifically in marriage counseling, but students may earn their undergraduate degree in social work, psychology or another related area. In addition to teaching students about the foundations of psychology and social work, these degree programs provide education in numerous areas directly related to marriage counseling, such as social psychology, cognitive psychology, sexuality, sociology and interpersonal relationships. Most bachelor's degree programs require completion of relevant internships or clinical practice prior to graduation.

Success Tip

Stand out as a student. Students applying to these competitive graduate programs need to present themselves as top candidates. Maintaining a high grade point average, participating in academic clubs and volunteering for local organizations can help students gain the competitive edge they need to secure a spot in these master's programs.

Step 2: Earn a Master's Degree in Marriage Counseling

A master's degree is the minimum education needed to become a marriage counselor. Master's degree programs fully educate students in social science-related areas of marriage counseling, often offering courses in areas such as adolescent and family counseling, cultural diversity, couples therapy, family systems sociology and marriage counseling ethics. Marriage counseling master's degree programs also place great emphasis on applied clinical experience and research, with students often having to complete numerous credit hours of clinical research and internships to earn their degree.

Step 3: Gain Clinical Experience as a Marriage Counselor

Marriage counseling licensure requirements vary from state to state. States mandate the completion of a certain number of hours of supervised marriage counseling work experience before granting licensure. These requirements sometimes exist independently of any clinical practicum credits accrued during completion of master's degree programs and are measured in weeks or hours, depending on the state. The standard supervised clinical requirement for marriage and family therapists is two years.

Step 4: Become a Licensed Marriage Counselor

A written exam is always required to obtain licensure, and classes and exams on ethical standards may also be required, depending on the state. Some states have their own licensing exams, while others utilize a standard exam provided by the American Association for Marriage and Family Therapy Regulatory Boards. After completing the required educational prerequisites, clinical work experience and exams, aspiring marriage counselors can apply for a state license. This is the final required step before beginning a career as a marriage counselor.

Success Tips

Earn additional credentials. Earning additional credentials through optional certification programs can help a marriage counselor stand out in the field. For example, the National Board of Certified Counselors offers an optional certification known as the National Certified Counselor (NCC) credential.

Join a professional organization. Professional organizations, such as the American Association for Marriage and Family Therapy, can greatly benefit a marriage counselor in the industry. These organizations offer continuing education options and networking opportunities.

Step 5: Complete Continuing Education

Almost all states require the completion of continuing education credits to maintain or renew a marriage counselor license. While exact rules and regulations differ from state to state, most licenses expire on an annual or biannual basis and require completion of approximately 30 continuing education units for renewal. Many states have lists of approved topics or course providers that are accepted towards fulfillment of these requirements.

Another option for continuing education is to earn a doctorate in marriage and family therapy. A doctoral degree can expand career opportunities into academia and research.

Success Tip:

Attend lectures and workshops. Workshops and lectures can help marriage counselors stay on top of relevant research and other industry trends. Attending these lectures and workshops may also count toward the required continuing education units needed for license renewal.

Aspiring marriage counselors must first earn a bachelor's degree, followed by a master's degree in marriage counseling, then they should gain experience and become licensed.

How to do Couples Counseling

Conflict is a part of relationships. It's simply that since no two people are exactly the same, you won't see the world the same way. That's why there are many, many different couples counseling techniques.

Couples' counseling is an important tool if those conflicts are starting to jeopardize the relationship as a whole. An occasional argument is probably healthy, but if it's all the time, it's a source of stress and unhappiness.

Conflict cannot always be avoided in relationships because no two people are exactly alike, so learning how to deal with conflict ensures a successful and healthy union. Relationship challenges arise in different ways, and being able to communicate with your partner is an integral part of a healthy relationship. Functional communication leads to better understanding between you and your partner, and understanding is the key to a successful union.

(1) Gottman Method

Gottman Method Couples Therapy has the benefit of three decades of research and practice in clinical settings with more than three thousand couples. The Gottman Method uses couples counseling techniques to increase affection, closeness, and respect. These techniques help you resolve conflict when you feel like you're at an impasse. You and your partner learn to understand one another and to discuss problems calmly.

The Gottman Method of couples counseling shows you how to build love maps, which help you learn about your partner's psychological world by mapping your partner's worries, stresses, joys, hopes, and history. Fondness and admiration are strengthened by expressing respect and appreciation for each other. This is a method of couples therapy that allows you to state your needs, and it stresses conflict management rather than conflict resolution.You and your partner learn to speak honestly about your aspirations and convictions. Trust and commitment to a lifelong relationship are reinforced.

(2) Narrative Therapy

One of the couples counseling techniquess, narrative therapy, seeks to separate the problem from the person by externalizing issues of concern. A therapist will ask you to describe your problems in narrative form, and then help you to rewrite the negative parts of the story. By acknowledging a problem doesn't define a person but is something a person has, you gain a new perspective on the situation. Narrative therapy helps you view your problem from different angles: culturally, politically, and socially. By stating negative issues in the narrative form, you become the dynamic in the story. The dynamic has the ability to change the story. Narrative therapy allows you to explore the past to bring to light negativities that otherwise remain hidden. By exploring conceptions and behaviors, you gain insight into facts that have been troubling you and your partner. Thus, you find new ways to deal with your problems, effectively rewriting the narrative of your relationship.

(3) Emotionally Focused Couples Therapy

Emotionally focused therapy was developed by Dr. Susan Johnson. This type of marriage counseling was first developed for couples, but it has proven useful for family counseling as well. Dr. Johnson's method is used worldwide in hospitals, clinics, private practices, and training centers. Although emotionally focused therapy is helpful in most situations, it especially should be considered if depression is a suspected culprit of relationship woes.

Typically a short-term approach, emotionally focused therapy has three main goals. It encourages the expansion and reorganization of key emotional responses. It seeks to secure a tight bond between you and your partner. The therapy repositions each partner's stance during interactions and creates new, beneficial interactions in your partnership. Emotionally focused therapy has been found to move 70 to 75% of relationships from a troubled state to a state of recovery. Significant improvement has been realized for 90% of couples using this therapy.

(4) Positive Psychology

Positive psychology emphasizes positive emotions, character strengths, and constructive institutions to promote the notion that happiness is derived from various mental and emotional factors. Positive psychology helps you identify happy moments as they happen rather than notice those moments in retrospect. Through this type of therapy, you learn to focus on positive emotions and to live in the present moment. Many couples find positive psychology liberating and joyful. Specialists believe perception dictates happiness from one event to another. Some people can't identify emotions as they arise but can see them clearly in hindsight. One technique uses beepers or pagers. The therapist beeps clients to remind them to record the experiences the clients are currently having. Clients expand upon these entries in a journal detailing the previous day. This practice conditions you to enjoy moments as they are experienced.

(5) Imago Relationship Therapy

Imago Relationship Therapy combines spiritual and behavioral couples counseling techniques with western psychological techniques of therapy to expose unconscious components that help you choose your mate. In this way, you and your partner are equipped to relate to each other in positive, caring ways. The therapist views the couple's conflict as a solution to the situation rather than the problem. Examination of the conflict is the key to finding a solution to disharmony.

Emotional discord in a relationship is often expressed as dissatisfaction, criticism, or anger. This forces you to seek comfort from people outside your relationship. Imago Relationship Therapy examines the root of negative emotions and behaviors to find the cause of severed communication between you and your partner. Acknowledgment that each partner is communicating differently helps resolves problems. Partners learn that disagreements aren't signs of love loss but are normal occurrences in relationships that can be resolved through communication.

(6) Analyzing the Ways you Communicate

The inability to communicate in healthy ways is the basis for the majority of problems in a relationship. Conflicts are bound to arise in partnerships, but by learning to communicate your positions clearly, you can turn conflict into a constructive discussion. Communication is a skill that requires conscious effort. What may seem clear to you may not always be fully understood by your partner. It's important for you to speak your mind rather than to expect one another to read moods and body language, which are open to misinterpretation.

Analysis of the methods you and your partner use to communicate offers insight into misinterpretation. A therapist can guide you toward functional forms of communication that alleviate misunderstandings. Learning new ways to communicate can seem unnatural at first but will help you and your partner to support and nurture each other.

(7) Exploring Unconscious Roots of Problems

Some couples counseling techniques take a psychodynamic approach to therapy. The purpose is to bring the unconscious roots of a problem to the surface, whether the problem belongs to one or both partners. This form of couples counseling is most useful when irrational patterns of reacting exist. The belief of a psychodynamic counselor is that significant life events and childhood experiences shape peoples' behavioral tendencies. Such experiences may create an unfulfilled need or a distorted view of reality that leads to dysfunctional behavior. Insight into these events serves to change perceptions, and functional patterns of behavior are realized.

Situations, such as childhood abuse or an unfaithful parent, can lead to unreasonable expectations in a relationship. Unreasonable expectations sometimes cause irrational distrust or jealousy. During couples counseling, the therapist explores major past experiences in order to change distorted perceptions and eliminate irrational reactions to current events.

(8) Enhancing Intimacy to Promote Closeness

Couples therapy is helpful regardless of whether problems exist in your relationship. Couples therapy isn't just limited to deflecting or solving problems; it also promotes closeness and intimacy in a partnership. Counselors help couples enrich their lives by aiding the development of friendship and ways to show affection. By providing exercises to increase mutual support, therapists teach couples how to overcome existing issues and how to make relationships resilient. Learning how to tackle challenges without the aid of therapy is as important as overcoming any problems you are experiencing presently.

Seeking counseling that encourages intimacy is helpful for couples having difficulties in a relationship. Undergoing this type of counseling before making a major commitment is beneficial to the future of your relationship. Some couples find this sort of therapy helpful in an existing relationship that is devoid of problems.

(9) Individual Counseling

Individual counseling is recommended when one partner is unwilling to undergo therapy or as a precursor to couples therapy. If both partners are not able to seek help with methods of communication, couples counseling can be ineffective. A common issue with individual therapy arises with the client's right to privacy. Some therapists insist their clients waive their rights to privacy before the therapist will work with partners individually. The best outcome can be expected when both partners are committed to counseling, even if they aren't firmly committed to the relationship. For a counselor to have a good idea of what is causing conflict, each partner should attend sessions together or separately.

Relationship Education

Relationship education promotes practices and principles of premarital education, relationship resources, relationship restoration, relationship maintenance, and evidence-based marriage education.

Examples

The National Council on Family Relations focuses on preparing professionals in family life education, a prominent approach to relationship education.

In 2006, the U.S. Department of Health and Human Services began funding significant multi-year demonstration projects through the Administration for Children and Families to expand the availability of marriage education classes in more than 100 communities nationwide. This project, known as the "Healthy Marriage Initiative," was designed to improve the well-being of children by providing tools and education to strengthen marriages and families.

Jeffry H. Larson conducted several studies on marriage and relationship education, including a review of three widely used premarital inventories - Focus, Prepare, and Relate.

Studies

Relationship Education for Premarital Couples

A multi-year federal study, known as the Building Strong Families Program, and 2010 meta-analysis of 47 studies found that relationship education "does not improve relationship quality/satisfaction" for unmarried couples.

"Previous studies have asserted that premarital education programs have a positive effect on program participants. Using meta-analytic methods of current best practices to look across the entire body of published and unpublished evaluation research on premarital education, we found a more complex pattern of results. We coded 47 studies and found that premarital education programs do not improve relationship quality/satisfaction when unpublished studies are included in the analysis, although studies that follow couples past the honeymoon stage to detect prevention effects are rare. In contrast, premarital education programs appear to be effective at improving couple communication, with studies that employed observational measures rather than self-report measures producing large effects. Still, given the mixed, modest results, there is ample room and a real need to improve the practice of premarital education."

Building Strong Families Program

Between 2002 and 2011, Mathematica Policy Research conducted the Building Strong Families Program study for the U.S. Department of Health and Human Services, Administration for Children and Families, "to learn whether well-designed interventions can help couples fulfill their aspirations for a healthy relationship, marriage, and a strong family."

The study specifically evaluated the impact of relationship education classes delivered to more than 5,000 low-income, unwed couples at 12 locations in seven states. "The intervention featured up to 42 hours of multi-couple group sessions led by trained facilitators, focusing on skills that, according to earlier research, are associated with relationship and marital stability and satisfaction."

In May 2010, Mathematica reported findings from a 15-month follow-up of program and control group participants:

- BSF had no effect on whether couples were still together 15 months after they had applied for the program, when data from the eight BSF programs are combined. At this point, 76 percent of BSF couples were still romantically involved, compared with 77 percent of control group couples. Similarly, BSF and control group couples were equally likely to be married to each other at that time (17 and 18 percent respectively) and to be living together, whether married or unmarried (62 percent for both research groups)."
- Fifteen months after they applied for the program, BSF and control group couples reported being equally happy in their romantic relationships, with average ratings of 8.4 and 8.3 respectively on a 0-to-10 relationship happiness scale. Similarly, BSF and control group couples gave very similar ratings of supportiveness and affection in their relationships, with average support and affection scale values of 3.5 on a 1-to-4 scale for couples in both research groups. In addition, BSF had no overall effect on how faithful couples were to each other.
- When results are averaged across all eight programs, BSF did not improve couples' ability to manage their conflict. Couples in both research groups reported similar levels of use of constructive conflict behaviors, such as keeping a sense of humor and listening to the other partner's perspective during disagreements. Similarly, there was no difference between the research groups in the avoidance of destructive conflict behaviors, such as withdrawing when there is a disagreement or allowing small disagreements to escalate. In addition, when results are averaged across all programs, BSF had no effect on how likely couples were to experience intimate partner violence. Similarly, when results are averaged across all programs, BSF did not improve co-parenting or increase father involvement. BSF and control group couples reported that their co-parenting relationships were of equally high quality. In addition, at the 15-month follow-up, couples in both research groups were equally likely to report that fathers were living with their children, spending substantial time with them, and providing them with substantial financial support.
- The Baltimore BSF program [Loving Couples, Loving Children] had negative effects on couples' relationships. BSF couples were less likely than control group couples to remain romantically involved, 59 percent versus 70 percent. Baltimore BSF couples reported being less supportive and affectionate toward each other than control group couples did. In

addition, women in the Baltimore BSF program were more likely than women in the control group to report having been severely physically assaulted by a romantic partner in the past year, 15 percent compared with 9 percent. Baltimore BSF couples also rated the quality of their co-parenting relationship lower than control group couples did and reported that BSF fathers spent less time with their children and were less likely to provide them financial support than control group fathers were.

Relationship Education for Married Couples

Several studies, notably the Supporting Healthy Marriage Project funded by the U.S. Department of Health and Human Services, Administration for Children and Families, a meta-analysis by Hawkins and Ooms and a five-year impact report by Peluso, Eisenberg and Schindler found that relationship education provided statistically significant benefits for married couples.

The emerging evidence suggests that MRE [marriage and relationship education] programs can work for low-income populations as well as for those who are economically better off. The evidence from a new meta-analysis of 15 program evaluations (including three randomized control trials) shows that MRE programs can have positive, moderate size effects on low-income couples' relationship outcomes, at least in the short run. However, the largest and most rigorous study of low-income, unmarried couples produced mixed results and shows there is still much to learn. Across nearly all the studies reviewed for this Report, MRE improves communication—a core, essential relationship skill—as well as other measures of relationship quality. There is also some initial evidence that MRE for low-income couples can decrease divorce rates, reduce aggression, and improve children's problem behaviors.

Supporting Healthy Marriage Study

In August 2012, Manpower Development Research Corporation (MDRC), a nonprofit, nonpartisan social policy research organization, reported that a federally funded, multi-year, random assignment, control group study known as the Supporting Healthy Marriage Project found high levels of consumer satisfaction among 4,989 adults participating in relationship education courses based on the work of PREP Inc., PAIRS Foundation and John Gottman at sites in Florida (Orlando), Kansas (Wichita), Pennsylvania (Reading and Bethlehem), Texas (El Paso and San Antonio), New York (Bronx), Oklahoma (Oklahoma City), and Washington (Shoreline and Seattle). A 12-month report on the program's impact found:

Couple practices communication skills during PAIRS Foundation relationship education class in Florida.

- The SHM program produced a consistent pattern of small positive effects on multiple aspects of couples' relationships. Relative to the control group, the program group showed higher levels of marital happiness, lower levels of marital distress, greater warmth and support, more positive communication, and fewer negative behaviors and emotions in their interactions with their spouses. The consistency of results across outcomes and data sources (surveys and independent observations of couple interactions) is noteworthy.
- Compared with individuals in the control group, program group members reported experiencing slightly less psychological and physical abuse from their spouses. Men and women in the program group reported less psychological abuse in their relationships, and men in the program group reported that their spouses physically assaulted them less often, compared with their control group counterparts.
- Men and women in the program group reported slightly lower levels of adult psychological distress (such as feelings of sadness or anxiety) than their control group counterparts.
- The program did not significantly affect whether couples stayed married at the 12-month follow-up point.

How to Guide Clients for a Healthy Relationship

1. Be Intentional

Be intentional and figure out the truth about your relationship. Think through all aspects of your relationship—your feelings and thoughts, the other person's feelings and thoughts, and the external context. If you notice yourself flinching away from a certain aspect of reality, this is the time to double down your focus and really get at the truth. The things you flinch away from, the truths you don't want to acknowledge to yourself, are likely to be the ones that will most undermine your relationship in the future. It's better to face the truth squarely in the face right now and address it rather than let it sabotage your relationship in the long run.

2. Avoid Failing at their Mind

One of the biggest dangers in close relationships is assuming the other person is exactly the same as you in their feelings and thoughts, and thus failing at their mind. This is something that's so easy to flinch away from, as our emotional self just doesn't want to accept that the person we're so close to is actually different from us—sometimes very different. I know I made this mistake, and it cost me dearly in the past. So how to avoid it?

3. Use Tell Culture

Use Tell Culture. Tell Culture is a communication strategy where you are open and honest with close people in your life about your feelings and thoughts, about what's going on with you, lowering your private barrier and being vulnerable and authentic. Tell them information about yourself that you think they would want to know.

For example, if you want a hug, you should tell the other person that you would enjoy a hug. However, for Tell Culture to work, it's really important for you not to expect that the other person will hug you. You are responsible for telling them about your needs and desires, and they are then free to act as they choose based on their own needs and desires.

4. Remove Communication Barriers

For open and honest communication to work, you need to remove communication barriers. Figure out your individual communication preferences and then compromise on something that works well for both of you.

5. Practice Emotional Attunement

As you communicate with each other, don't listen only to what the other person is saying, also listen to the emotions underneath the words. Notice whether the other person seems stressed, frazzled, sad, frustrated, confused, pleased, glad, joyful, etc.

Pay attention to the tone of the voice, body language, and what is not being said as well as the content of the words. Such emotional attunement will level up your ability to understand the other person, and respond in ways that lead to happy and long-lasting relationships.

6. Check in on your Relationships

This is a magic-bullet solution to so many relationship problems. Schedule systematic meetings to talk about the state of your relationship and what can be improved. For the process, you can follow this science-based questionnaire or come up with your own approach to the relationship check-in.

For example, my wife and I have a relationship check-in every two weeks. We first talk about what we appreciated most about each other during the last two weeks. Then we discuss what can be improved in our relationship, and how to do so. We then finish up with gratitude to each other for doing the relationship check-in and have some delicious chocolate to reward ourselves. It's done wonders for improving our relationship.

7. Trust Others

All of these strategies will help you build up trust, what research shows is key to having happy, lasting relationships. Always keep in the back of your mind a personal evaluation of the level of trust in the relationship. How much do you trust the other person to act in ways that both match your mental model of that person? How much do you trust that person to have your back? If you want an intentional relationship, do things to build up trust and gather information about the other person's trustworthiness. Exhibit vulnerability and openness, share secrets, and be generous in your offers to compromise. If the other person shows themselves trustworthy, then be more committed to the relationship. If they do not, then re-evaluate your own level of commitment, as the relationship likely will not work in the long term.

8. Respect Boundaries and Privacy

A key aspect of showing trust is allowing each other to set boundaries and permitting privacy.

Technological developments make it so easy for us to track each other and to be in constant communication. However, permitting each other to have a private space and avoiding pushing the other person to do things they would prefer not to do helps a lot in creating sustaining happiness in relationships. Respecting boundaries and permitting privacy will do wonders for building up mutual trust.

9. Have Healthy Conflicts

Surprise, conflicts can be healthy in relationships. If you go into a relationship expecting never to fight, you'll lose out on great relationships because the first fight might well lead to the end of the relationship. Instead, learn strategies for healthy conflict resolution, and talk about them with your relationship partner before the fact.

Start any conflicts by highlighting how you care about the other person and the relationship. Talk about both the facts and how you feel about them. Avoid the blame game and instead be as generous as you can be in interpreting the other person's actions. Be open to changing your mind if you discover you made the mistake and apologize quickly and profusely. Avoid focusing on the past and instead orient toward better behavior in the future. At the end of any conflict, focus on reconnecting and rebuilding emotional bonds strained by the conflict. My wife and I found these techniques to be so helpful in resolving tensions between us.

10. Meet your Own Goals

Remember that you are in the relationship for yourself, not the other person. So meet your own goals first in any relationship. Be intentional and consider what you want from the relationship as you evaluate it in your own mind and heart. Don't allow the other person's needs and desires to overwhelm yours. Play by the rules of Tell Culture and be honest and open with the other person in the relationship about your needs and desires, and encourage that person to be honest and open with you. Otherwise, you risk building up resentment and frustration both for yourself and the other person in the relationship, and subverting the possibility of a happy and long-lasting relationship.

11. Compromise

Balance getting your needs met with meeting the other person's needs. Seek a mutually beneficial compromise on any areas of disagreement. The ability to compromise is key to happy and lasting relationships. Today's society emphasizes individuality, but for any relationship to work, we need to get out of the self-centered shell and put ourselves in the shoes of the other person, understanding their perspective, thoughts, and feelings. That makes compromise much easier. My wife and I make compromises for each other all the time, big and small, and that's how we keep our relationship strong.

12. Don't Fight Against Change or Diversity

People change and relationships change all the time. This is not something to mourn, but just a fact of life, to be acknowledged and celebrated. Sometimes, relationship needs to become more diverse for both people to remain happy. So consider the possibilities of non-traditional relationships such as polyamory and others. At other times, people who were right for each other earlier are no longer right for each other. To ensure mutual happiness, it's important to let each other go at that stage. The key is to be intentional and pursue your own goals in any relationship you are in.

How to Guide your Clients to Deal with Disappointment in a Relationship

It's common to feel disappointed in a relationship. If you had certain expectations that were not met, you may feel let down. However, disappointment is not unusual and can be addressed in a healthy manner. To start, manage your emotions in the aftermath. When you are feeling calm, talk to the other person about the issue. From there, work on a way to move forward together.

Part 1. Coping in the Moment

1. Manage your emotions. In the direct aftermath of any kind of disappointment, it's vital to manage your emotions. Whether they're good or bad, you need to feel what you're feeling in order to process.

- Give yourself a day or so to experience your emotional reaction to a disappointment. You do not have to act on your emotions at this point and, in fact, it is better not to act. You can simply let yourself take a low-key day to consider how you're feeling. Do you feel angry? Confused? Afraid? It can help to do some light journaling, jotting down how the disappointment made you feel and why.
- It's important to experience your emotional reaction to an event. Your emotions can offer you insight into how much something meant to you. If you feel mildly annoyed that your boyfriend cancelled date night at the last minute, your disappointment may not be that significant. However, if you find yourself emotionally distraught all day over the let down, there may be deeper issues at play you need to address.

2. Try not to take it personally. While disappointment feels very personal, it's not always a shot at you. Even if it's hard, try not to take another person's failings personally. It's not necessarily a reflection of how that person feels about you.

- Many people have a tendency to internalize life's setbacks. You may feel if someone else let you down, you must have done something to bring that letdown on yourself. You may feel like you deserved it, attracted it, or are simply not good enough to have experienced a different outcome.
- Try to silence that negativity. This narrows your point of view in a way that's simply inaccurate. There are a variety of factors that may lead to a disappointment. The person who let you down did not, in all likelihood, intend to hurt you. Before personalizing disappointment, consider all the factors involved.
- Remind yourself that you don't know all the facts. If your best friend suddenly cancelled a lunch date, this can sting. However, maybe she was having a bad day. Maybe she experienced a disappointment of her own, at work or in her personal life, that affected her mood. She may have just wanted some time alone. While it's okay to be disappointed, try to remember you don't have all the facts.

3. Put yourself in the other person's shoes. Oftentimes, when we're feeling disappointed we may jump to thinking something like, "I would *never* do that to someone." However, is this really true?

In reality, we all disappoint others all the time, whether intentionally or not. If you know anything about the other person's situation, put yourself in his or her shoes. How would you have acted?

- For example, say you're feeling let down because your friend went out to a club without you. The two of you had plans to stay in and watch a movie, but a co-worker your friend wants to get closer to invited her out at the last minute. If you initially feel hurt, you may feel your friend acted poorly and that you would never cancel plans like this.
- However, put yourself in the other person's shoes. Say your friend is new to the city. She's been struggling to make friends for a while and feels somewhat lonely. Maybe, given her situation, she was worried about alienating this co-worker and missing the opportunity to aggregate to a new community. Also, consider yourself from your friend's point of view. Are you the kind of person who enjoys going to clubs? If not, your friend may have decided it was better not to invite you as she figured you wouldn't have fun.

4. Be kind to yourself. If you're feeling a great deal of pain after a disappointment, it's important to practice some self care. Anger, resentment, and sadness are common emotions to experience in the wake of disappointment. Do something nice for yourself. Watch a movie, take a warm bath, or order take out. Giving yourself a small treat can help you better regulate your emotions.

Part 2. Talking Things Out

1. Write down your thoughts. If you're unable to get over a disappointment, it's important you talk things out with the other person. Having a conversation about how someone hurt or disappointed

you can be stressful. You should try writing your emotions out ahead of time. This way, you'll have your thoughts somewhat organized going into the conversation.

- Try to write down what you're feeling. After spilling your thoughts out onto the page, consider how you can best articulate them. Reword your thoughts a bit, trying to phrase them in a way that would make sense to another person.
- Also, keep in mind what you want to accomplish. Do you want an apology? Do you want the person to explain his or her actions? Do you want this person's behavior to change in the future? The answers to these questions can help guide your writing.

2. Have empathy. If you're going to have a difficult conversation with someone, enter the conversation with empathy. This will prevent you from coming off as combative during a discussion. Try to consider the other person's perspective as much as you can. Be open to listening to their side and genuinely considering it. Remember, the point of a conversation is to resolve a dispute and not to win it. There are two sides to every story and it's important to be open to the other person's side.

3. Go into the conversation without expectations. You should abandon any expectations you may have going into the conversation. If you expect things to go a certain way, you may feel disappointed or frustrated when they turn out differently. Allow the discussion to unfold naturally. Remember, you don't know how the other person will feel. It's unproductive to make assumptions ahead of time.

4. Use "I"-statements. "I"-statements are statements phrased in such a way to emphasize personal feeling over objective truth. When you use an "I"-statement, you make your feelings the main point of a sentence. You are not blaming or judging a person for his or her actions. You are simply stating how those actions made you feel and why.

- "I" statements have three parts. They begin with "I feel," followed by the emotion you're feeling. Then, you explain the action that lead to that emotion. Finally, you say why you felt the way you felt.
- The point of an "I"-statement is to minimize blame and judgement. You are not saying the person on the listening end is objectively wrong. Instead, you're saying how their actions made you feel. For example, if you're talking to your boyfriend and feeling frustrated, you may be inclined to say something like, "You make us late to every social event we go to and that's incredibly disappointing to me."
- The above statement can easily be rephrased into an "I"-statement. Your boyfriend will feel less judged, and may be more inclined to listen to your perspective if he understands he hurt your feelings. Using an "I"-statement, you could say something like, "I feel disappointed when we end up late to social events because I feel like you don't respect my need to see my friends."

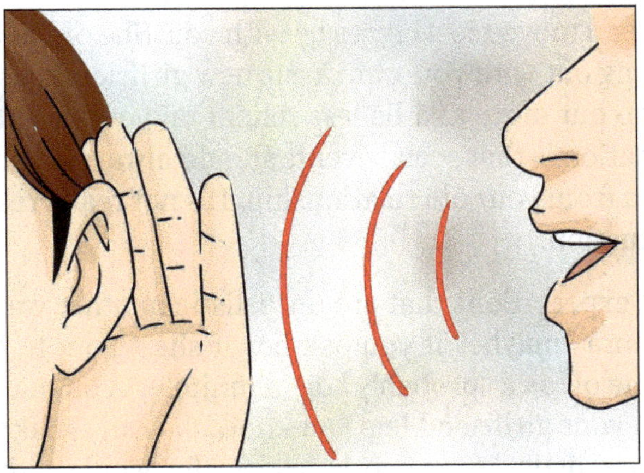

5. Listen to the other person's point of view. Once you've explained how you feel, listen to the other person's perspective. Even if someone's behavior has disappointed you, there may be reasons for

that behavior you do not understand. Try to be positive. The point of a conversation is to heal and move forward.

- Returning to the above example, maybe your boyfriend simply does not understand timetables like you do. He may say something like, "I guess I didn't realize 7 o'clock meant exactly 7 o'clock. When I go out with friends, we have a general time to meet and then people just kind of trickle in."
- The problem is an issue of communication rather than disrespect. Your boyfriend simply interprets timing for social events more loosely than you. In the future, you can try to be clearer about when precise timing is important.

Part 3. Moving Forward

1. Examine your expectations. Sometimes, people may have unrealistic expectations of a relationship. If you're feeling disappointed with someone a lot, look at your own expectations. Can you see where your expectations may not be particularly realistic?

- Oftentimes, we may have expectations that seeped in from past relationships. For example, say your last girlfriend moved to a city to be with you. She did not have a lot of friends there and, as a result, hung out with you a lot. Your new girlfriend has been living in this city for a while. She may go out more and be less reliant on you for entertainment and socialization. If your expectation is that social events should always be done together, this may be a leftover expectation from your old relationship. It's not really reasonable, considering your new girlfriend's situation.
- You may also have expectations that are unrealistic in other ways. For example, your girlfriend may give you a "maybe" if you ask her if she wants to hang out later. For you, a "maybe" might come off as a "probably" or "definitely." You may find yourself consistently disappointed when your girlfriend lets you know she can't make it that night. Maybe your expectations are unrealistic. Many people, especially people with busy schedules, may simply be unable to commit some days. You can start seeing a maybe as a maybe, and expect that you may have to find something else to do that night.

2. Reframe your expectations as necessary. If your expectations do seem unreasonable, work on reframing them. Sometimes, future disappointment is less likely if you learn to accept certain things about another person.

- Let's return to our above example. Your new girlfriend is clearly more independent. She has her own life, her own career, and her own social circle. She may not be the type of person who needs a significant other to feel complete.
- In this case, try to reframe what you expect of a romantic relationship. In this relationship, you may not spend all your free time together. Your girlfriend may go out with just her friends a few times a week. Try to accept this is just your girlfriend's personality and it's not a bad thing. Next time she's going out for drinks with coworkers, you may be less disappointed that she can't come over and watch a movie after work.

3. Try again. Once you've reframed expectations, try again but on a different track. In any relationship, you have to be willing to compromise. If a friend, family member, or romantic partner has a different way of doing things, it's important that you allow that person that freedom. Proceed with the relationships, but with your expectations slightly altered. Try to be more accepting of the other person's perspective and more direct in how you communicate your own wants and needs.

4. Consider the big picture. When reeling after disappointment, it can be easy to get stuck going over one incident. However, keep the big picture in mind. Is this relationship important to you? Does this person bring more good into your life than bad? If so, the occasional disappointment is not worth getting upset over. Everyone disappoints another person on occasion, and it is usually unintentional. Try to let go and move forward.

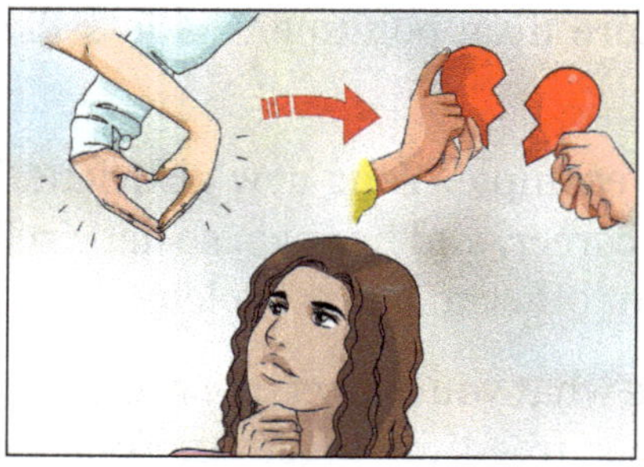

5. Accept that relationships change. Oftentimes, a sense of disappointment in a relationship comes from the fact relationships change. It's possible you're holding on to past expectations that are no longer feasible. Try to allow a relationship to evolve and acknowledge that changes do not necessarily indicate something is wrong with a relationship.

- For example, look at a typical romantic relationship. At the beginning of the relationship, you and your partner may have sex more often, spend more time together, and talk constantly. As the relationship progresses, things may calm down some. You may have moments of silence, for example, and sex may be less frequent than how it was before.
- It's natural for the excitement of a new romance to fade with time. The intensity of the first few months of dating usually calms down. This is not necessarily a bad thing. While you may miss the thrill of a new romance, there are benefits to falling into a routine. The two of you are more comfortable together. You're both able to be yourself. Try to look at your changing relationship as an indicate of stability rather than stagnancy.

How to Guide your Clients to Deal with Stress in Relationships

Every relationship has rough spots. When that time comes, there's no need to freak out. Every relationship has its ups and downs: stress is just as natural a part of it as are more enjoyable moments.

We all go through hard times at work or with our friends or family. Or perhaps, stress can come from a misunderstanding with your partner. This is the normal course of life: you shouldn't let it impact your relationship and your own emotional well-being.

Method 1. Dealing with External Sources of Stress

1. Isolate the source of stress. This could come from either outside your relationship (work, family, financial issues) or from within. If the source of stress is not the relationship itself, don't let stress spoil your private life. Learn how to manage so that it doesn't seep into conversations with your partner.

- When stress comes from outside the relationship, the best solution is to nip the problem in the bud. For example, if your dissatisfaction with a job is putting strain on your relationship, consider getting a new job instead of letting it affect your well-being.

2. Make a priority check. If your relationship matters more to you than the source of stress or the fact that you're stressed, then you should focus on your own and your partner's well-being.

- Make it clear to your partner that your relationship is still more important than anything else. For example, you can say: "I'm sorry I'm going through a difficult time at work, and that this is putting a strain on us. You know you're what matters the most to me."

3. Deal with stress together, not as individuals. See you and your partner as a team facing a difficult time and looking for a solution together. Put your ego in a corner and think through problems by asking yourself "What can we do?" rather than "What can I do?"

- If the stress is due to your partner's dealing with a hard situation, sympathize and show your active encouragement. As part of a team, you're called to play the role of helper and comforter.
- Make it clear that you are committed to the relationship no matter what problem you and your partner are dealing with. Stress tests the strength of any relationship. If you want to stay together despite the hardships, state it clearly.

4. Work on your communication skills. Most relationship problems have their origin in the partners' failure to express their concerns and emotions straightforwardly. The first skill a couple needs as a team is to speak clearly, honestly and respectfully.

- Don't hold back your feelings. Silence is another source of strain in itself, and will only build up tensions. Express all your concerns and emotions, but do it in a way that is sincere and not judgmental. Go for positive statements like "I'm feeling" or "I think that", rather than questions ("Why did you?") or negative sentences ("I didn't like").
- Humor is a great for relieving tension. Making a joke about a difficult situation, or seeing its funny side, will give both of you a positive outlet for your stress and help you put things into perspective. However, make the joke on you or the difficult situation, not on your partner.

5. Face financial problems together. Money is one of the first causes of stress in a relationship. If debt, unemployment or related issues are putting a strain on your life as a couple, you should be open about it and look for a solution together.

- Look for professional financial advise without feeling ashamed. It is an adviser's job to help people through difficult times: you situation is just one of many they've dealt with.
- Don't blame each other for being in dire straits. Accusing your partner of spending money on a night out instead of saving it for more important stuff will only increase tension.
- Don't hide anything from your partner and make sure he or she is just as transparent. Discuss honestly how money loss has changed your life and how this is making you feel.

6. Remember that work shouldn't take over your relationship. Jobs take up a large part of everyone's life and energy. However, work-related stress can often affect a couple's well-being. This doesn't mean you have to keep it all to yourself. Share it with your partner and find stress-relieving activities together.

- Don't ever use your job as a term of comparison with your partner. You might have similar or completely different occupations, but it's never a good idea to measure your professional success or failures against your partner's.
- Allow yourself and your partner some quality time off work. You can actually cheat on your job, every once in a while, as a sign that what you truly care about is not in your office.

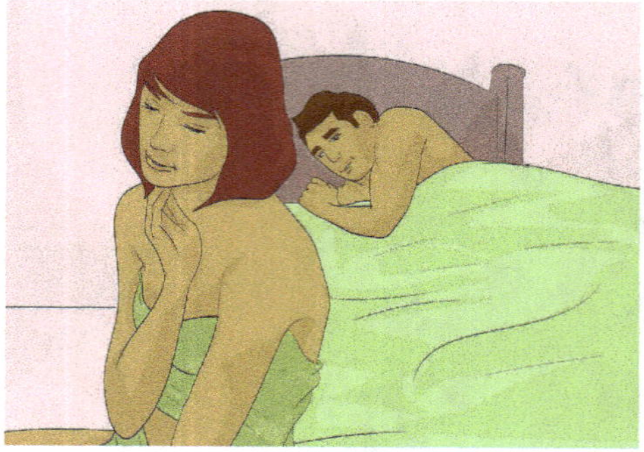

7. Learn to cope with illness as a couple. Chronic pain or an unexpected disease can put a lot of strain on a relationship. If this happens, remember that illness can change your habits but you're still the same people as before. Deal with the change together, and don't forget that partners are there to help each other especially in this case.

- If you're in pain, don't hold back. Let your partner know how this is affecting your life and making you feel. You can't expect your partner to read your mind: express yourself clearly and don't be afraid to ask for help.
- Keep having sex, if your own or your partner's condition still makes it possible. Being ill doesn't mean you should give up on life as a whole. Make the most of what you can still enjoy.

8. Listen. In stressful times, you might tend to focus on your own problems and feelings. This can make you forget that your partner can help you only if you let him or her speak.

- Don't dismiss what they say: think their advice through and show gratitude for the effort.

Method 2. Overcoming Relationship Trouble

1. Isolate the problem in your relationship. If the stress comes from difficulties in your relationship,

make a distinction between such problems and the relationship itself. You shouldn't let one single difficulty affect the entire relationship.

- Find out what doesn't work in the relationship and address this specific issue by using what does work as a point of strength.

2. Give responses, not reactions. What makes a reaction different from a response is its intensity and emotional subtext. Think your answers through. If one implies anger, sarcasm, accusations, it's a reaction. This will only turn communication into a table-tennis match where the goal is to win rather than to find a solution. However, a team always plays on the same side.

- Don't phrase your comments as judgments or blame your partner out of spite. This can only lead to further stress and misunderstanding. You can do this by focusing on future objectives rather than past actions. If you were disappointed at your partner's not doing the dishes, seize the next occasion to ask them to do the dishes, without mentioning the fact that they didn't in the past.
- Don't invalidate your partner's opinions just to win an argument. Proving yourself right might be good for your ego, but it never makes a team stronger.
- Understand that, when we're angry, communication follows war patterns: aggression and defense. You should avoid both, and try to bring the conversation back to equal terms. Express ideas as positive statements, without using them as weapons or shields.

3. Discuss rough reactions openly. If your partner's tone becomes aggressive or judgmental, point it out gently and ask what was behind the message. What we say is usually not as important as why we said it. This will help you address the original source of stress, instead of spending time arguing over a harsh reply.

- Be tolerant if your partner has a bad reaction. If this happens repeatedly, point out this is not a useful discussion. It will never lead to a solution but only further stress.

4. Respect your partner and expect respect in return. This is the golden rule of any relationship. Showing each other respect through what you say or do will decrease the level of stress, whether the source is external or internal.

- Respect means having equal power in a relationship. What you say or do is just as important as what your partner says or does. Stress, instead, always derives from a power imbalance. For example, one of the two partners might be overly controlling or submissive.

5. Trust and accept your partner as he or she is. Stress can also come from failed expectations. If that is the case, the problem is in what you expected rather than what your partner failed to provide. You chose your partner with all his or her faults and weaknesses, not as a fixer-upper. Love rests on acceptance and confidence.

- A consequence of acceptance is forgiveness. Your partner might have done something wrong. If your relationship is what matters the most, however, you should let go instead of holding grudges.

6. Be open to negotiation and surrender. Every relationship calls for continuous rearrangements

and resolutions of conflicts. If communication is smooth and equal, negotiation happens as a natural process. This also means you should know how to lose or give up an argument, if that's not what matters the most to you.

- Surrendering doesn't mean passively fulfilling all of your partner's wants. It is an active choice to downsize your desire to be always right or in control. However, this must also occur on a mutual basis. If you're the one surrendering all the time, there is a power imbalance that needs to be worked out.

7. Talk to a relationship coach if needed. If you think stress has had too much of an impact on your relationship and that you and your partner cannot solve the problem on your own, discuss with him or her the possibility of seeking professional help. A counselor will offer an objective point of view and help you focus on strategies to attack the problem.

- If your partner doesn't want to join you, you can still meet with a counselor or therapist on your own. This will provide an external outlet where you can take out your stress and get professional advice on how to deal with it.

Method 3. Dealing with Stress on your Own Time

1. Take some time off from your partner. A relationship can often feel like a 24/7 job. However, it's perfectly natural to feel like spending some time on your own every once in a while, especially if you're under pressure. Find activities you can do by yourself without fearing that this would hurt the relationship.

- If you're stressed because you feel you've lost your own self in a relationship, try to reaffirm your individuality and what makes you a unique person.
- In fact, enjoying some independence will make you go back to your partner as a stronger individual. Missing each other is good: it helps you realize why your partner is so important and cherish the time you spend together.

2. Find alternative ways to decompress. Especially if stress comes from outside the relationship, you should find external outlets so that you can unload the burden before being with your partner.

- This depends on what way is best for you to decompress: sport works for many people. However, you might prefer reading, going out more often, walking or meditation.

3. Exercise. There is no better way to take the burden off your chest than shake it away with physical activity. Even if you're not exactly the sporty kind, you can be sure that sweating out stress will lessen its impact on your relationship.

- The kind of activity depends on what you find most effective as a stress relief. Cardio activities like jogging, swimming or cycling can give you a chance to clear your mind. Or, you might prefer kickboxing or martial arts if you need to take out nervous tension. Yoga can work best if you wish to combine sport and meditation.

4. Share problems with your family and friends. Your partner shouldn't be the only person you unload your stress with. Talk to close friends or family members about your concerns and ask for their advice and sympathy.

- If you talk to someone in your family, make sure they would be supportive. You don't want family issues to add more stress to what you're already going through.
- Friends who care about you but are personally uninvolved in what's causing you stress could be the best people to talk to. For example, if stress comes from your job, look for support from a friend who's not linked to it.

Conflict Resolution

Conflict resolution is conceptualized as the methods and processes involved in facilitating the peaceful ending of conflict and retribution. Committed group members attempt to resolve group conflicts by actively communicating information about their conflicting motives or ideologies to the rest of the group (e.g., intentions; reasons for holding certain beliefs) and by engaging in collective negotiation. Dimensions of resolution typically parallel the dimensions of conflict in the way the conflict is processed. Cognitive resolution is the way disputants understand and view the conflict, with beliefs, perspectives, understandings and attitudes. Emotional resolution is in the way disputants feel about a conflict, the emotional energy. Behavioral resolution is reflective of how the disputants act, their behavior. Ultimately a wide range of methods and procedures for addressing conflict exist, including negotiation, mediation, mediation-arbitration, diplomacy, and creative peacebuilding.

The term *conflict resolution* may also be used interchangeably with *dispute resolution*, where arbitration and litigation processes are critically involved. The concept of conflict resolution can be thought to encompass the use of nonviolent resistance measures by conflicted parties in an attempt to promote effective resolution.

Theories and models

Dual concern model

The dual concern model of conflict resolution is a conceptual perspective that assumes individuals' preferred method of dealing with conflict is based on two underlying themes or dimensions: concern for self (assertiveness) and concern for others (empathy).

According to the model, group members balance their concern for satisfying personal needs and interests with their concern for satisfying the needs and interests of others in different ways. The intersection of these two dimensions ultimately leads individuals towards exhibiting different styles of conflict resolution. The dual model identifies five conflict resolution styles/strategies that individuals may use depending on their dispositions toward pro-self or pro-social goals.

Avoidance Conflict Style

Characterized by joking, changing or avoiding the topic, or even denying that a problem exists, the conflict avoidance style is used when an individual has withdrawn in dealing with the other party, when one is uncomfortable with conflict, or due to cultural contexts. During conflict, these avoiders adopt a "wait and see" attitude, often allowing conflict to phase out on its own without any personal involvement. By neglecting to address high-conflict situations, avoiders risk allowing problems to fester or spin out of control.

Yielding Conflict Style

In contrast, yielding, "accommodating", smoothing or suppression conflict styles are characterized by a high level of concern for others and a low level of concern for oneself. This passive pro-social approach emerges when individuals derive personal satisfaction from meeting the needs of others and have a general concern for maintaining stable, positive social relationships. When faced with conflict, individuals with a yielding conflict style tend to harmonize into others' demands out of respect for the social relationship.

Competitive Conflict Style

The competitive, "fighting" or forcing conflict style maximizes individual assertiveness (i.e., concern for self) and minimizes empathy (i.e., concern for others). Groups consisting of competitive members generally enjoy seeking domination over others, and typically see conflict as a "win or lose" predicament. Fighters tend to force others to accept their personal views by employing competitive power tactics (arguments, insults, accusations or even violence) that foster intimidation.

Conciliation Conflict Style

The conciliation, "compromising", bargaining or negotiation conflict style is typical of individuals who possess an intermediate level of concern for both personal and others' outcomes. Compromisers value fairness and, in doing so, anticipate mutual give-and-take interactions. By accepting some demands put forth by others, compromisers believe this agreeableness will encourage others to meet them halfway, thus promoting conflict resolution. This conflict style can be considered an extension of both "yielding" and "cooperative" strategies.

Cooperation Conflict Style

Characterized by an active concern for both pro-social and pro-self behavior, the cooperation, integration, confrontation or problem-solving conflict style is typically used when an individual has elevated interests in their own outcomes as well as in the outcomes of others. During conflict, cooperators collaborate with others in an effort to find an amicable solution that satisfies all parties involved in the conflict. Individuals using this type of conflict style tend to be both highly assertive and highly empathetic. By seeing conflict as a creative opportunity, collaborators willingly invest time and resources into finding a "win-win" solution. According to the literature on conflict resolution, a cooperative conflict resolution style is recommended above all others. This resolution may be achieved by lowering the aggressor's guard while raising the ego.

Conflict Resolution Curve

There are many examples of conflict resolution in history, and there has been a debate about the ways to conflict resolution: whether it should be forced or peaceful. Conflict resolution by peaceful means is always a better option. The conflict resolution curve derived from an analytical model offers a peaceful solution by motivating conflicting entities. Forced resolution of conflict might invoke another conflict in future.

Conflict resolution curve (CRC) separates conflict styles into two separate domains: domain of competing entities and domain of accommodating entities(Image of CRC). There is a sort of agreement between targets and aggressors on this curve. Their judgements of badness compared to goodness of each other are analogous on CRC. So, arrival of all conflicting entities to some negotiable points on CRC is important before peace building. CRC does not exist (i.e., singular) in reality if the chance of aggression of the aggressor is certain. Under such circumstances it might lead to apocalypse with mutual destruction.

The curve explains why nonviolent struggles ultimately toppled repressive regimes from power and sometimes forced leaders to change the nature of governance. Also, this methodology has been applied to capture the conflict styles in Korean Peninsula and dynamics of negotiation process.

Conflict Management

Conflict management refers to the long-term management of intractable conflicts. It is the label for the variety of ways by which people handle grievances—standing up for what they consider to be right and against what they consider to be wrong. Those ways include such diverse phenomena as gossip, ridicule, lynching, terrorism, warfare, feuding, genocide, law, mediation, and avoidance. Which forms of conflict management will be used in any given situation can be somewhat predicted and explained by the social structure—or social geometry—of the case.

Conflict management is often considered to be distinct from conflict resolution. In order for actual conflict to occur, there should be an expression of exclusive patterns which explain why and how the conflict was expressed the way it was. Conflict is often connected to a previous issue. Resolution refers to resolving a dispute to the approval of one or both parties, whereas management is concerned with an ongoing process that may never have a resolution. Neither is considered the same as conflict transformation, which seeks to reframe the positions of the conflict parties.

The role of culture is not always fully appreciated and must be taken into account. In a piece on "the ocean model of civilization", Prof Nayef Al-Rodhan argues that greater transcultural understanding is critical for global security because it diminishes 'hierarchies' and alienation, and avoids dehumanization of the 'other'.

Counseling

When personal conflict leads to frustration and loss of efficiency, counseling may prove helpful. Although few organizations can afford to have professional counselors on staff, given some training, managers may be able to perform this function. Nondirective counseling, or "listening with understanding", is little more than being a good listener—something every manager should be.

Sometimes simply being able to express one's feelings to a concerned and understanding listener is enough to relieve frustration and make it possible for an individual to advance to a problem-solving frame of mind. The nondirective approach is one effective way for managers to deal with frustrated subordinates and coworkers.

There are other, more direct and more diagnostic, methods that could be used in appropriate circumstances. However, the great strength of the nondirective approach lies in its simplicity, its effectiveness, and that it deliberately avoids the manager-counselor's diagnosing and interpreting emotional problems, which would call for special psychological training. Listening to staff with sympathy and understanding is unlikely to escalate the problem, and is a widely-used approach for helping people cope with problems that interfere with their effectiveness in the workplace.

How to Guide Clients to Resolve Conflicts in a Relation

1. Be Direct

Sometimes people don't just come out and plainly state what is bothering them, and instead choose more indirect ways of expressing their displeasure. One partner may speak to the other in a way that is condescending and implies underlying hostility. Other times, partners may mope and pout without really addressing an issue. Partners may also simply avoid discussing a problem by quickly switching topics when the issue comes up or by being evasive. Such indirect ways of expressing anger are not constructive, because they don't give the person who is the target of the behaviors a clear idea of how to respond. They know their partner is irritated, but the lack of directness leaves them without guidance about what they can do to solve the problem.

2. Talk about how you Feel without Blaming your Partner

Statements that directly assault your partner's character can be especially damaging to a relationship. If a man frustrated by his girlfriend's jealousy says "You're totally irrational." he is inviting her to become defensive, and this can shut down further conversation. A more constructive strategy is to use "I statements" and pair them with "behavior descriptions."*I statements* focus on how *you* feel, without blaming your partner, and *behavior descriptions* focus on a specific behavior your partner is engaging in, rather than a character flaw. For example, this man might say, "I get irritated when you claim I'm flirting with someone during an innocent conversation." These tactics are direct, but don't impugn your partner's character.

However, it should be noted that these direct negative tactics *can* be constructive — in some situations. Research has shown that for couples with relatively minor problems, blaming and rejecting one's partner during a conflict discussion was associated with lower relationship satisfaction over time and tended to make problems worse. For couples with *major problems*, a different picture emerged: Blaming and rejecting behaviors resulted in less satisfaction immediately following the conflict discussion, *but over the long term*, the problems improved, and this led to increases in relationship satisfaction.

3. Never Say Never (or "always")

When you're addressing a problem, you should avoid making generalizations about your partner. Statements like "You *never* help out around the house," or, "You're *always* staring at your cell phone" are likely to make your partner defensive. Rather than prompting a discussion about how your partner could be more helpful or attentive, this strategy is likely to lead your partner to start generating counterexamples of all the times they were, in fact, helpful or attentive. Again, you don't want to put your partner on the defensive.

4. Pick your Battles

If you want to have a constructive discussion, you need to stick to one issue at a time. Unhappy couples are likely to drag multiple topics into one discussion, a habit renowned conflict researcher John Gottman calls "kitchen-sinking." This refers to the old expression "everything but the kitchen sink," which implies that every possible thing has been included. When you want to solve personal problems, this is probably not the strategy you take with yourself. Imagine that you wanted to think about how to incorporate more physical exercise into your daily routine. You would probably not decide that this would also be a great time to think about how to save more money for retirement, organize your closet, and figure out how to deal with an awkward situation at work. You would try to solve these problems *one at a time*. This seems obvious, but in the heat of the moment, a fight about one topic can turn into a complaining session, with both partners trading gripes. The more complaints you raise, the less likely it is that any will actually get fully discussed and resolved.

5. Really Listen to your Partner

It can be very frustrating to feel like your partner is not paying attention to you. When you interrupt your partner or assume that you know what they're thinking, you're not giving them a chance to express themselves. Even if you are confident that you know where your partner is coming from or know what they're going to say, you could still be wrong, and your partner will still feel like you're not listening.

You can show your partner that you're paying attention by using *active listening* techniques. When your partner speaks, paraphrase what they say — that is, rephrase it in your own words. This can prevent misunderstandings before they start. You can also *perception-check,* by making sure that you're interpreting your partner's reactions correctly. For example, "You seem irritated by that comment — Am I right?" These strategies both prevent misunderstandings and show your partner that you're paying attention to them and care about what they're saying.

6. Don't Automatically Object to your Partner's Complaints

When you're criticized, it's hard not to get defensive. But defensiveness doesn't solve problems. Imagine a couple arguing because the wife wants her husband to do more chores around the house. When she suggests that he do a quick clean-up after he gets ready to leave in the morning, he says, "Yes, that would help, *but* I really don't have time in the morning." When she suggests that he set aside some time on the weekend, he says "Yes, that could be a way to schedule it in, *but* we usually have plans on weekends, and I have work to catch up on, so that won't work." This "yes-butting" behavior suggests that her ideas and views are not worthwhile. Another destructive, defensive behavior is "cross-complaining," when you respond to your partner's complaint with one of your own. For example, responding to "You don't clean up enough around the house" with "You're a neat freak." It's important to hear your partner out and really consider what they're saying.

7. Take a Different Perspective

In addition to listening to your partner, you need to take their perspective and try to understand where they're coming from. Those who can take their partner's perspective are less likely to become angry during a conflict discussion.

Other research has shown that taking a more objective perspective can also be helpful. In one study, researchers staged a simple marital quality intervention, asking participants to write about a specific disagreement they had with their partners from the perspective of a neutral third party who wanted the best for both members of the couple. Couples that engaged in this 20-minute writing exercise three times a year maintained stable levels of marital satisfaction over the course of the year, while couples who didn't showed declines in satisfaction.

8. Do not show Contempt for your Partner

Of all of the negative things you can do and say during a conflict, the worst may be *contempt*. Gottman has found that it is the Number One predictor of divorce. Contemptuous remarks are those that belittle your partner. This can involve sarcasm and name-calling. It can also include nonverbal behavior like rolling your eyes or smirking. Such behavior is extremely disrespectful, and implies that you're disgusted with your partner.

Imagine that one partner says, "I wish you took me out more," and the other responds, "Oh yes, the most important thing is to see and be seen and overpay for tiny portions of food at some rip-off restaurant. Could you be more superficial?" Or one partner says they're too tired to clean up, and the other responds, "I'm sure you're *sooo* exhausted after a long day of chatting at the water cooler. I've been busting my butt all day, and you just get home and sprawl out on the couch, staring at your smartphone like a teenager." This kind of contempt makes it impossible to engage in a real discussion and is likely to elicit anger from your partner, rather than an attempt to solve the problem.

9. Don't get Overwhelmed with Negativity

It can be hard not to respond to a partner's bad behavior with even more bad behavior. But indulging that urge will only make the conflict worse. When couples engage in what Gottman and his colleagues calls "negative affect reciprocity," they trade more and more heated insults and contemptuous remarks. And as the conflict goes on, the negativity escalates. So *how much is too much* negativity? In his research, Gottman found that the magic number is a *5 to 1 ratio*: Couples that maintained a ratio of five positive behaviors (e.g., attempts at good-natured humor, warmth, collaboration) to each negative behavior were significantly less likely to be divorced or separated four years later.

10. Know when it's Time for a time-out

If you see yourself falling into negative patterns and find that either you or your partner are not following the tips above, consider taking a time out from your argument. Even a short break for a few deep breaths can be enough to calm hot tempers.

Enmeshed Relationships

Typically people in enmeshed relationships have a hard time recognizing that they're actually in an unhealthy relationship, Doing so means acknowledging their own emotional issues, which can trigger anxiety, shame and guilt, he said.

However, making this realization is liberating. It's the first step in making positive changes and focusing your attention on building healthy relationships, including the one with yourself.

In the therapy work, therapists does a "cost-benefit analysis" with clients. They helps them understand that they have much more to lose by staying in an enmeshed relationship *as is* than by making changes and finding healthy relationships.

Rosenberg shared these signs, which are indicative of enmeshed relationships.

- You neglect other relationships because of a preoccupation or compulsion to be in the relationship.
- Your happiness or contentment relies on your relationship.
- Your self-esteem is contingent upon this relationship.
- When there's a conflict or disagreement in your relationship, you feel extreme anxiety or fear or a compulsion to fix the problem.
- When you're not around this person or can't talk to them, "a feeling of loneliness pervades [your] psyche. Without that connection, the loneliness will increase to the point of creating irrational desires to reconnect."
- There's a "symbiotic emotional connection." If they're angry, anxious or depressed, you're also angry, anxious or depressed. "You absorb those feelings and are drawn to remediate them."

How to Guide your Clients to Break Free of Relational Enmeshment

Enmeshed relationships leave a legacy of heartache and manipulation. But that legacy can be changed if we are willing to open our eyes. It is possible to break the pattern of enmeshment and break through to freedom—to that place where we are able to give and receive true love."

Here are some steps we must take to break free of relational enmeshment and discover the freedom of true love:

Steps

1. Realize the patterns in your family of origin, especially if one or more of your parents was alcoholic or addicted in some way. Often, an addict's family enables them to continue destructive behavior, protecting them from the consequences of it by rescuing them, covering for them, and so on.

2. Ask a trustworthy friend for feedback about your relational patterns. When we're stuck in enmeshment, we sometimes refuse to listen to people outside the situation, who notice our unhealthy patterns. To break free, we must be willing to listen to feedback about how our rescuing and enabling actually hurts the person we're trying to help. We must be open to the truth about ourselves.

3. Acknowledge the truth that pleasing and helping others, even when it keeps them from taking

responsibility, makes us feel good. But ultimately, it's detrimental to us, to the other person, and to our relationship. Facing the truth (that your helping is actually hurting) is an essential step toward healing.

4. Decide to trade the false love of enmeshment for real love. "True love is not wrapped up in a drive to rescue, overprotect, control, or manipulate. It genuinely wants the best for the other person," Clinton writes in his book Break Through. "It is grounded in our heart's desire to cherish, honor, and treasure another person simply because of who they are. True love offers a safe place to be you; it's not driven by a desire to rescue or a need to perform. True love values the other person for who they are and celebrates healthy separateness."

5. Communicate clear boundaries to the other person. For example, if you're in the habit of writing checks to your adult child when they get into financial trouble, this enabling behavior is keeping them from growing up. But warn them ahead of time that you won't be doing that anymore. Tell them they will need to be responsible for their own financial life. Expect some resistance—after all, you've taught them an unhealthy dependence on you. Changing the pattern begins with clear communication.

6. Enforce those boundaries. An enmeshed person's goal, whether they realize it or not, is to protect the other person at all costs—even if they're protected from the consequences of their own bad behavior. A person with healthy boundaries allows others to experience the consequences of their own choices. But it may not be easy to stick to your guns. Be strong. Get help from a trusted friend or counselor to help you enforce the new boundaries you are setting.

How to Guide your Clients to Overcome an Infatuation

When infatuation turns from euphoria to obsession, it's time to make some changes. Constantly thinking of someone can take a toll on your life and cause an unhealthy mental situation. One can overcome this infatuation by getting back to reality, refocusing your thoughts, and getting help and support.

Method 1. Getting Back in Touch with Reality

1. Analyze the person's faults. It's difficult to see nothing else about a person you're infatuated with except for how amazing they are. However, no one is perfect and everyone has flaws--even them. Make a list of their negative qualities to bring you back down to reality.

- Finding these flaws will likely take some time. Engage with the person outside of your regular circumstances or spend more time with them than usual. Chances are, seeing them outside of your typical scenario will show you a different, and unflattering, side.
- If, after significant time and effort, you are unable to find any flaws, this could signal an especially problematic obsession. Seek professional help immediately.

2. Look at patterns of infatuation. Have you been through this before? Chances are, if you're infatuated with someone now you have likely been in the same situation previously. If obsession is a common occurrence in your life, tell yourself so.

- For example, when your feelings get overwhelming, remind yourself that this is just something that you do. It's not indicative that you are completely in love with or can't live without this person, it's simply a tendency you have. Coming to terms with that may make you realize that your infatuation is just a habit.

- Try journaling. Journaling can help you organize your thoughts and better understand patterns of infatuation in your life.

3. Give it time. The saying "time heals all wounds" is popular because it is true. Look back at other moments in your life when you were obsessed or infatuated with someone or something. Ask yourself how you feel about them today. Chances are you are completely over it and over time, this infatuation will be a distant memory, too.

Method 2. Refocusing your Thoughts

1. Think about someone else. Telling yourself to simply stop thinking about your infatuation won't work. In fact, there's proof that trying to stop these thoughts typically makes them worse. Instead, encourage your mind to think about something else: another person.

- Think about the person you are already in a relationship with, if you are in one. Ponder a time when you felt really close and connected to the person. You'll likely find that experiencing these feelings kick the other person out of your head.
- If you aren't in a relationship, focus on someone else you admire, such as a close friend, a family member, or a respectable member of your community.

2. Use your imagination. Play mind games with yourself whenever you start to obsess about the

person. Occupying your brain with a clever trick can stop the thoughts and encourage you to think about something else.

- For instance, imagine your mind as a small room that has a person with a broom living in it. Think about the person sweeping away dust and dirt on the floor of that room whenever your infatuation enters your mind. Continue this game until the floor is completely clean and the thought leaves your brain.

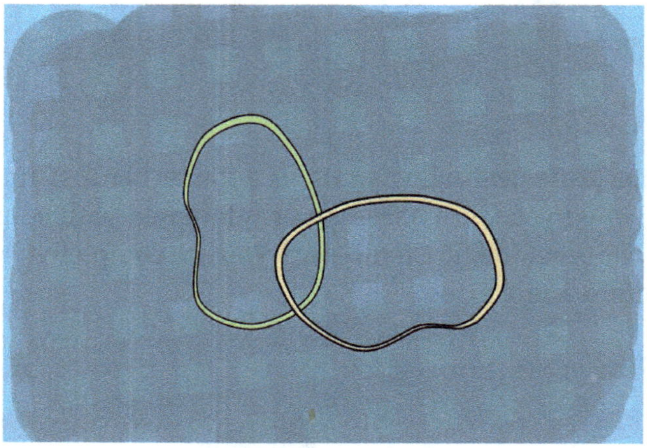

3. Snap out of it, literally. Pain is an excellent deterrent and can be used to stop obsessive thoughts. Wrap a rubber band around your wrist and snap it against your skin whenever you begin to think of your infatuation. Eventually you'll likely associate the pain with these thoughts and stop.

- Don't snap the band too hard. The sensation should be mild.
- Combine the wrist snap with a visual aid, like a red light or a stop sign. Think of these images whenever the unwanted thoughts pop up.

4. Distract yourself. Redirect your brain by engaging in an activity. You'll get your mind off of what you're infatuated with while enjoying yourself at the same time.

- For example, read a book, watch your favorite television show, exercise, or call someone. The positive feelings you generate from these activities will likely eventually replace the negative ones you feel over your infatuation.

Method 3. Getting Help and Support

1. Talk to a professional. Patterns of infatuation are often indicative of a love addiction. You may have become dependent on the feelings you experience when you are infatuated with a person so you tend to repeat the same behaviors. A therapist may be able to help you break the cycle.

- Ask your friends, family members, or a doctor for recommendations. Look online for names if you don't feel comfortable asking those you know.

How to Guide your Clients to Save a Relationship

Part 1. Figuring Out the Problem

1. Consider when things went wrong. If you are at a critical juncture, you can probably figure out when things started going off the rails, even just a little bit. Think about when the problem started, so you can figure out how to approach the discussion with your partner.

- You may easily pinpoint one major reason, such as you or your loved one was unfaithful, and that changed the dynamic of the relationship.
- More often, you may not be able to find one major reason, but rather, a series of reasons for why things aren't working out. A lot of little things can start to add up. For example, maybe he's spending too much time with his friends, or you never make time for each other. Alternatively, maybe you're both stressing at work.

- Maybe you're growing incompatible. If you've been together for a long time, it's possible that you've become different people over the course of the relationship.
- If you're unsure where to begin, consider taking a relationship quiz that can help you assess how healthy your relationship is.

2. Decide whether you should try to save it. Sometimes, a relationship can't be saved, especially if the other person isn't willing to put in any work. If only one of you wants to save it, that's not going to work out. Also, if your relationship is abusive in any way, either physically or emotionally, then you probably shouldn't try to save it.

3. Pick a good time to talk to your partner. You should pick a time when you have few distractions. Also, it should be in a private space, so that you won't be overheard. In addition, try to choose time when you both aren't overly emotional. You should try to have a calm, rational discussion, putting emotion to the side.

4. Talk with your partner. If your marriage or relationship is need of saving, it's likely that your partner already knows a problem exists. However, if you haven't talked about it, you need to start

the discussion. It's best to do so when you are calm and level-headed, so that you can actually discuss rather than shout at each other.

- It's important to not just talk, but to listen and hear what your partner has to say about what's going on in your relationship. You can show you're listening by summarizing what your partner has to say to show you've understood what he or she has said. You can also ask questions that show you've heard what the person has said and that you want to know more.
- When you're bringing up the problem, focus on "I" statements rather than "you" statements. For example, you could say, "I'd really like to discuss what's been going on with our relationship," rather than "You're making our relationship a mess."

5. Come up with a list together. While discussing your relationship, work on a list together. Figure out what you both think the problems are in your relationship, and discuss how it started. It may be hard to have an open discussion, but it's important to get both of your points of view on where the relationship went wrong. In addition, you can use help from educational websites to help identify what's healthy about your relationship and what's not.

- For instance, a healthy relationship is one where you are both your own, independent people and you respect each other's personalities and boundaries. You are interested in what the other person is doing, and you encourage one another.
- Unhealthy relationships, on the other hand, are where one or both of you is not happy with who the other person is, and you are pressured to change the person. You may also feel controlled or manipulated, or you may be the one doing the manipulating.

6. Focus on patterns. Rather than blaming each other, consider how patterns from each of you has

led to problems. For instance, maybe you consistently forget to call home when you're going to be late, and your partner then gets upset when you don't show up. Consequently, you punish him or her the next time by not calling home, which is a cyclical pattern. When you bring it up, focus on how to solve the problem, such as "I will try to be better about calling home, if maybe you can forgive me the few times that I forget. Or maybe you can send me a text near the end of the day, so I will be more aware of what time it is."

Part 2. Figuring Out How to Deal with the Problem

1. Consider counseling. If you are at the point where you are trying to save your relationship, it's a good idea to call in professional help. A counselor can help you decipher what problems you have, especially if you can hardly stand to be in the same room together anymore.

2. Be honest with each other. Being honest is a kind of vulnerability, and by being honest with your partner, you show that you trust him or her. Try opening up about what you're thinking and feeling. When you're vulnerable, you're inviting your partner in and asking him or her to be equally as honest. However, it's important to continue using "I" statements to tell how you feel instead of blaming the other person.

- For example, when you're talking to your partner, you shouldn't say, "You never put me first." Rather, you should say, "I sometimes feel neglected in the relationship." That way, you're telling how you feel rather than pointing fingers.

3. Work collaboratively. Instead of each taking one side of an argument, it's important to work together. You should work together in your relationship, treating each other as teammates rather than enemies. However, you also need to work together when trying to solve problems. That means first agreeing on what the problem is.

- Once you agree on what the problem is, you also need to talk about what both you are concerned about underneath the surface. That is, you may both have an idea in mind of what winning looks like, but if you are both set on winning, no one will win in the end. Instead, discuss why you want the solution you do.
- You should also look for common ground in the problem and the solution. That is, if you're disagreeing about who should do what housework, at least you agree that the house needs more attention. That's a starting place.

4. Discuss solutions. This step may be the hardest part, coming up with solutions you both can live with. That means agreeing on what you think the main problems are in the marriage and coming up with ways you can both work to make it better. Basically, you need to compromise. Blaming each other isn't going to help, as you've both contributed to the situation you're in.

- Compromising means you need to talk about what you both need and want in the relationship. This step is important, because then you can decide where you can both stand your ground and where you can both give a little. Compromising means giving in where you feel you can.
- It helps if these solutions are concrete. For instance, maybe you've decided one of your main problems is that you don't spend enough time connecting. The solution could be that

you agree to go on one date a week, plus you will try to spend lunchtime together at least three times a week.

- Maybe you're problems are partially financial. Sit down and agree on a budget moving forward, one that compromises on what you both value. For instance, if you're a saver and want to penny pinch every dime while your partner enjoys extravagant vacations, compromise by going on a more modest vacation every year that is within your budget.
- Portion out the household chores. One small thing that can become huge is if one person feels he or she is doing all the work at home. Have an open discussion about a fair division of the work, and try making a schedule to determine who will do what when.

5. Learn to forgive. If you're going to move forward, you're going to have to forgive each other for the hurts you've caused. That doesn't mean completely forgetting what happened or even saying what happened was okay. It does mean that you need to acknowledge the hurt it caused you. You need to realize that the other person makes mistakes, and both of you learned from that mistake. Finally, you need to accept that it happened and move on.

- Most mistakes stem from needs that a person wants to be met. Realizing that can help you learn from what happened.

6. Figure out what will happen moving forward. Once you've identified the problems and solutions, you need to both formally commit to the solutions. The solutions need to be concrete and ones you can both live with.

- If you find your solutions aren't working after a certain period of time, it's fine to revisit them and try something new.

7. Don't forget boundaries. Once you've made a plan about how to move forward, don't forget that you also need to set boundaries. Yes, you forgive each other for what's happened, but you can still put boundaries in place to keep the same mistakes from happening again.

- For instance, if one of you cheated after going to a certain club, it seems reasonable that that person should not return to that club. You could bring it up by saying, "Because of what's happened in the past, I don't feel comfortable with you going to the club. If you insist on going, that may be a deal breaker for me."

Part 3. Relearning How to Love Each Other

1. Think about why you got together. When you're in a dire situation where your relationship is failing, you may have forgotten why you got together in the the first place. Spend some time reflecting on what you liked about him or her in the first place.

- Maybe she could always make you laugh, or he made sure to call to see if you got home safely. Think about all the little things that you used to love about the other person. One way you can think about the past together is to look at old photos together.

2. Make sure you are both open to change. If your primary goal is to protect yourself in the

relationship from hurt and anger, you aren't open to change. Instead, you'll likely want to control your partner to enforce that protection, making your relationship negative and stagnant. On the other hand, if you're both willing to learn and grow together, your relationship can develop over time into something better. If only one of you is willing to change, it may not work.

3. Focus on what's good. Think about what you love about your partner. In fact, take some time each day to write down five things you love about your partner or are grateful for in your partner. Try to put those thoughts into words and actions by expressing gratitude towards your partner.

4. Find out each other's love languages. Everyone experiences love differently. Gary Chapman breaks this idea down into the five ways people experience love or the five love languages. If you've never taken the time to figure out each other's love languages, now is the time to do it. You can take quizzes online to figure out what your love language is.

- The first love language is words of affirmation, which means that you feel loved when you hear words that value you.
- The second love language involves service, meaning that you feel loved when someone gives of his or her time to help you out or to do chores around the house.
- The third love language is gifts. That means that you feel loved when you receive small (or large) tokens of appreciation from people who are close to you.
- The fourth love language is time. With this love language, you feel loved if a person spends time with you.
- The final love language is touch. In other words, you feel loved if a person is affectionate with you by kissing you, holding your hand, cuddling with you, or hugging you, for instance.

5. Apply the love languages. That is, in your interactions with each other, try to use the other person's love language to show that you care. If your partner's love language is service, try doing little things around the house to show you care or try taking his or her car to the wash. If your partner's love language is time, make sure to figure out ways to spend more time with the person on a regular basis.

6. Take time to connect. Just like when you first got together, you need to spend time together, just the two of you. You may think you know everything about your partner, but people can still surprise you even years later. Take time each day to talk to your partner and ask about his or her life, thoughts, and feelings.

- One way to learn something new about your partner is to try taking a class together, such as a cooking or dance class. You'll experience something new together and rekindle some of the old spark.

7. Enjoy hobbies together. Though tastes may change, you should make time to do something you

used to love doing together. If you used to love cooking Chinese food together, try it again. If you once trained for a half marathon but are now feeling too out of shape, commit to the challenge. By committing to something you enjoyed doing before, you'll rekindle some of the old passion you felt. However, it doesn't just have to be something you used to enjoy together. You can also try something new.

8. Get physical. That is, you need to remember to connect to each other through touch, not just sex. When you're together, hold each other hands, cuddle, or hug. Touch her arm while she's talking. Rub his knee while you're sitting next to each other. Touch is important in maintaining intimacy, and it can be lost to the daily grind over the years.

9. Keep communicating. Once you've started on this path, you may think you'll be able to fix your problems just by sitting down together once and talking about it. However, maintaining a relationship means constantly checking in with each other and talking about what's going on and how you're feeling.

- Communication is especially important when you feel yourself getting angry at your partner and wanting to be short with him or her. Instead of getting angry, take a moment to breathe. Once you've calmed down, take a moment to talk about why you are getting upset and what can be done about it.

Part 4. When Should you Try This

1. Try to save it if you're still in love. There was a reason you got together to begin with, a seed of love that kept you going this long. If you still feel that love, it's worth working to find a way to communicate and get in sync with each other again. Many loving relationships get off track from time to time. It will take work to restore it, but it's worth the attempt if you know in your heart that you care about this person.

2. Consider trying to save it if your significant other wants to. Maybe you're the one who is on the verge of giving up on the relationship, but your partner wants to keep trying. If you've been together for a long time, it might be worth giving it your all to try to save it. It might be possible to see your partner's love for you and have faith that even though you're going through a rough time right now, things can get better. Weigh the options and see if it's worth it to you to try for the sake of your partner.

3. Give yourself permission to stop trying when you're ready. No matter how good things used to

be, or how much one party wants the relationship to keep going, sometimes it's clear that it has to end. If you've already put in effort trying to save the relationship, and you no longer feel love or the will to try to reignite it, it's OK not to force yourself to keep trying. Don't spend months or years dragging it out and criticizing yourself for not being able to make it work. It's OK to choose happiness over self-sacrifice. When one person stops participating in the relationship, it's better for both people if it ends.

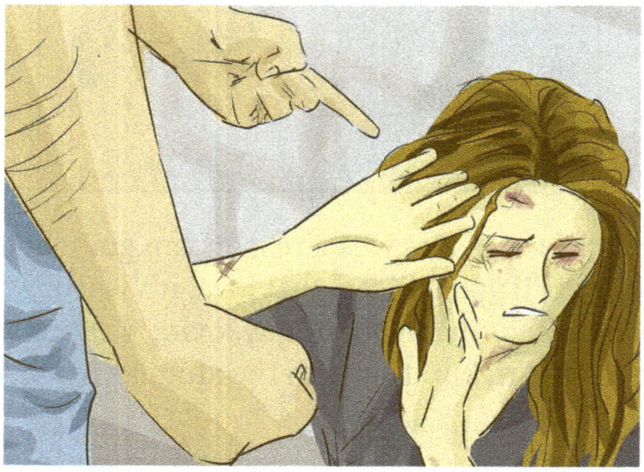

4. Don't try to save a relationship that's toxic or abusive. There's really no way to work on a relationship that's based on toxic patterns or abuse. No amount of working on communication techniques or trying to reignite the romance is going to make things better long-term. You may feel that you're getting something out of the relationship, but you have a lot more to gain by being free.

How to Guide your Clients to get out of a Bad Relationship

Part 1. Preparing for a Break-Up

1. Admit you're in a bad relationship. To get out of a bad relationship, the first step is to recognize that you're in one. It's easy to ignore the signs and keep living your daily life in a failing relationship, but no one should suffer like that. Everyone deserves to be happy.

- Write down the warning signs you feel are happening in your relationship. Review the list to get a clear picture of what is truly happening.
- Talk to a close friend or family member about your concerns to hear someone else's view.
- Know that you have the power to make a change and to get out of the relationship.

2. Arrange a place to go after the break up. Ask a trusted friend or family member if you can spend some time with them after you cut ties in the relationship. Having someone close to you provide support will help you feel better about your decision.

- If your relationship has had a history of abuse, it is important to let someone know your plans to help provide you with safety following the break up. You should also develop a safety plan for when you leave the relationship. This should include getting support from loved ones and domestic violence professionals, anticipating a change of heart and resisting the urge to stay, and having your things ready to go.

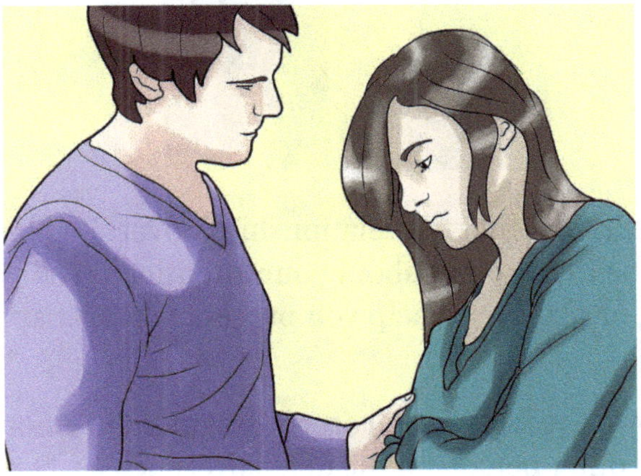

3. Create a plan of action. To be able to succeed at ending a bad relationship, you need to have a plan in place. Creating a plan of action can help you hold yourself accountable to follow through. The most successful plan is one with specific implementation intentions, or if/then statements.

- "If I start to miss my ex, then I will call a friend to go hang out."
- "If I begin to regret my decision, then I will write out a list of the reasons I left."
- "If I become depressed over the break-up, then I will seek out help."

Part 2. Ending the Relationship

1. Plan a time to talk with your partner. Prepare yourself for when you are going to end the relationship.

- Large social gatherings may create embarrassing scenarios for a break-up.
- Consider meeting in a quiet public space to avoid confrontations.

2. Tell your boyfriend or girlfriend that the relationship is over. Be blunt and direct. When ending a relationship, it is best to be to the point about your intentions. Tell your partner how you feel in person, rather than calling or texting, to help you process what is happening and show you mean what you are saying.

- Make sure you stick to the facts so you aren't caught up in emotions and use "I" statements to avoid putting the other person on the defensive, such as, "I have been unhappy with our relationship lately, and it's time to end things between us."
- Deliver the message in a calm, direct voice so your significant other knows you are serious about the decision: "I am breaking up with you."
- If you are afraid of your significant other having a violent reaction to the relationship ending, you should not meet in person or alone. In this case a phone call would be the better option.

3. Put distance between yourself and your new ex. Once you've ended the relationship, you will need to stay away from the person you left. Bad relationships are often mentally tough to leave; make it easier on yourself by ending contact with the person so you aren't tempted to get back together.

- Delete your ex on all social media accounts.
- Take your ex's phone number out of your phone.
- Go to different places for entertainment where you won't see your ex.
- Ask your friends not to talk about your ex to help you create distance.

Part 4. Moving On

1. Surround yourself with positive people. After getting out of a toxic relationship, it is important to surround yourself with the right kind of people. You need to be around someone who will build you up and remind you that you did the right thing.

2. Release your regrets. When a relationship ends, it's easy to fall into the trap of dwelling on what

you could have done better to change your ex. Know that no matter how much you think about the past, it won't change.

- Learn from the relationship rather than regretting it. Try to focus on what you want moving forward to help you stay positive and to move in the direction you want to go.
- Be kind to yourself. Try not to overthink the reasons why the relationship went bad. Focusing on the past will only hinder you from thinking about the future.

3. Forgive yourself. You shouldn't feel bad about a failed relationship. Many people beat themselves up for not seeing the signs of a bad relationship, but this kind of thinking will only make you feel worse.

- Forgive yourself by stating it aloud or writing it down.
- Remind yourself that everyone makes mistakes, and you can learn lessons from the failed relationship.

4. Remember who you were before the relationship started. It's easy to lose track of your true interests when you have been in a bad relationship. Now you have time to rediscover yourself revive your interests or seek new ones.

- Take a class in something you used to enjoy learning about.
- Join a club.
- Pick up a hobby from your past.

5. Ask for help. When it's too hard to process the break-up by yourself, you might need to have some help. Ask for help from friends or family; talk with people who are close to you when you are feeling down.

- Don't feel ashamed if you need to ask for help. Many people find themselves in the same place, and professional help gets them back on their feet.
- Use your family and friends for emotional support to help rebuild yourself after a bad relationship.

6. Contact local authorities for protective orders. If your ex is harassing or intimidating you, get in touch with the local police to request a restraining order. Reach out to shelters or support groups if you feel threatened or endangered.

How to Guide your Clients to Deal with Changes in your Relationship

Relationships naturally endure many changes, whether it's moving, starting a new job, spending time apart, getting married, or having children. While some changes can be difficult, there's no need to see change as a bad thing. By being adaptive and communicating regularly, you and your partner can endure changes in your relationship.

Part 1. Responding to Changes

1. Change your view on change. Change doesn't have to be a bad thing and many positive things can result from change. There's no need to assume the worst when change comes along. Instead, think of what positive things may result from change.

- For example, it can be hard to move, but think about the exciting parts of starting a new adventure together, exploring new places, and meeting new people.

2. Accept that you may be seeing your partner differently. If you feel like your partner has all of a sudden changed (especially for the worst), consider that your partner always had these traits, but you're seeing him or her differently now. Once the honeymoon phase is over, you may see your partner in a different light, and it may not always be pleasant. You may not want to immediate blame your partner for the changes and instead, recognize that your perception may have changed.

- if you're really bothered by something your partner does, recognize that it's your own annoyance that is bothering you, not your partner. Find ways to cope with your feelings of annoyance or upset, such as learning to tune out behaviors or taking deep breaths.

3. Allow for your differences. Sometimes one partner may change a viewpoint that changes the relationship, like about marriage or having kids. Don't take differences in views or beliefs personally. Just because you and your partner have different views doesn't mean that one is attacking the other. It doesn't mean that your approach is lesser than and there doesn't have to be a "best" and "worse." It just means that you disagree, and it's okay to accept those differences.

- It's okay to call some topics "off limits" if you know that they bring conflict with no resolution. Things like politics or religion can cause major disagreements with no obvious resolution. Agree not to discuss certain topics together.

4. Take some time off. If the change causes confusion or strong emotions, take some time away from each other and away from arguing. Make sure that you agree on the amount of time and that you use the time to think about the problem. Simply taking time away from each other will not solve the problem.

- For example, you might just need to take a 15 minute break in separate rooms, or you might agree to take a week to think things over separately and then meet to resume the discussion again at a set time and place.
- Do some digging and ask yourself why this change affects you so much. Is there something the change is triggering? Are there fears or worries? Figure out what is upsetting you or filling you with fear.

- For example, if you used to agree on having kids and now you disagree, take some time to figure out why your position is so important for you. Where are the fears from? Why is it that you feel so strongly? You may want to journal your thoughts and feelings.

Part 2. Communicating About the Changes

1. Give each other emotional support. Changes can be hard on both people in a relationship. Even if you're struggling, reach out and support your partner. Let your partner know that he or she is important to you and that you care about the relationship. Give affection, care, and respect, and express yourself through thoughtful words and gestures.

- Say, "This is hard, and I'm struggling. Yet, I want you to know I care about you and I want this relationship to work. I'm here and willing to support you."

2. Discuss the changes. Talk about how big changes affect each of you separately and how they affect the relationship as a whole. Let your partner express his or her feelings completely. It may not be an easy conversation and may extend to several conversations. However, it's important to communicate clearly with your partner when big changes occur.

- Be honest about how you feel. Use "I statements" to convey your feelings. For example, say, "I feel nervous and anxious about you starting night school. I feel like I'll see less of you, which makes me feel sad. At the same time, I'm proud of you and want you to pursue what makes you happy."

3. Listen to what your partner wants. While you may want to express your thoughts, needs, and feelings to your partner as soon as change comes up, take a step back and ask your partner about how he or she is experiencing the change. Listen intently and let your partner communicate his or her thoughts, feelings, and needs. Show your partner your care by being available to listen.

- Improve your listening skills by reflecting and restating what your partner says. For example, say, "I hear you saying that this change is hard on you too, and that you feel it's important to go through with this, even though it's difficult."
- Validate your partner's feelings. Say, "I can tell it's really hard for you to talk about your father's death, and you feel depressed. I can understand why this is so hard for you."

4. Keep your relationship in mind. When faced with changes, remind yourself how much you value your partner and your relationship. How much are you willing to let the changes affect your relationship? For example, if your partner gets a new job across the country, you may feel upset with him or her. Keep in mind your relationship and respond in ways that show that you are prioritizing your relationship.

- If you're upset, ask yourself whether it's worth making your partner "pay" for the changes, or whether it's better to keep things in perspective and value your partner.

5. Be flexible and willing to accept some ambiguity. When you are faced with changes, it is impossible to know what might happen and trying to identify and think about every detail of a situation can be paralyzing. Instead, prepare as well as you reasonably can for a situation, and then take a step back. Deal with the challenges that come your way one at a time and be flexible enough to adapt as needed.

- For example, if you and your partner have to spend some time apart because one of you gets a job that requires lots of travel, then you might anticipate some challenges. However, don't try to identify every single possible challenge ahead of time and work out solutions to each one in advance. Instead, work out solutions to a few of the big challenges that you might face and then focus on other challenges as they arise.
- For example, you could come up with a plan for known challenges, such as child care, managing household tasks while the other is away, and communicating. Having a plan for known challenges that you both agree on can help both of you feel like you have some structure even as you head into unknown territory.

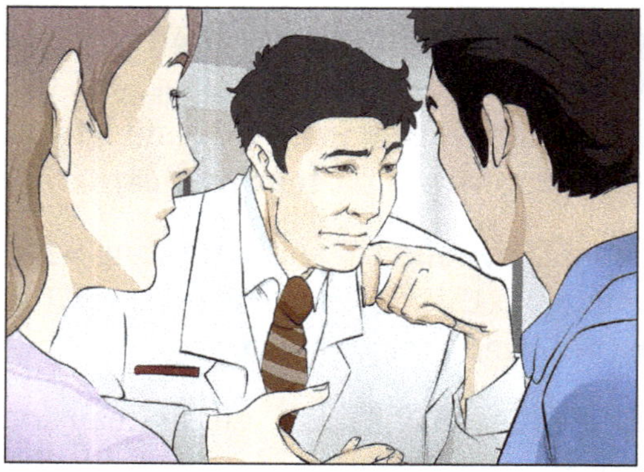

6. See a therapist. You may come to a point where you realize that your relationship needs intervention and therapy may be necessary to deal with the changes. A couples counselor can help you and partner improve your communication, and state your thoughts, feelings, and beliefs in truthful and meaningful ways. Especially in periods of transition and change, therapy can be an invaluable tool for getting through challenging times.

- You can also work on emotional avoidance and dysfunctional behavior in the relationship.

Part 3. Prioritizing the Relationship Through Times of Change

1. Be affectionate. Touch can provide support on physiological and psychological levels. Maintain touch with your partner through times of change. Hold hands, put your arms around each other, and show that you want to be close together.

- Maintain your sex life and prioritize having sex together. Scheduling sex doesn't sound sexy, but it can help you connect regularly.

2. Bring back old pleasures. If you're feeling disoriented by change, bring something old and familiar back into your relationship. Maintain a sense of normalcy (or nostalgia) by doing something you used to do together once again.

- Perhaps you enjoyed watching old episodes of "I Love Lucy" together when you first started dating. Invite your partner to watch an episode with you. Re-create a date you both enjoyed or eat a treat you have fond memories of together.

3. Try something new. Find an activity that both of you want to do and do it together. Even when change might feel bad, do something new that feels good. Doing something new together can ignite feelings of excitement and emotional intimacy.

- Go ice skating or spelunking. Try a new activity together such as golf or painting. Whatever it is, make it fun and appealing to each of you.

4. Plan regular date nights. Plan time to spend time together, just the two of you. This can be a

great way to reconnect and enjoy time together on a regular basis. Keeping your dates consistent can give you something to look forward to and a way to know that you can spend time meaningfully connecting.

- Avoid topics like finances and focus on reminiscing about when you were first dating, fond memories of your kids, and other pleasant memories.

5. Take a mini-vacation. You may want to take some time off from experiencing changes and have some time together, just the two of you. Take a weekend and go somewhere nice where you can spend time together, be affectionate, and enjoy each other's company. It can be nice to get away from pressures and deadlines and changes to just having time together.

- Get out of the house and away from the to-do lists. Go somewhere that brings you peace and calm and inspires connection with your partner.

Premarital Counseling

Premarital counseling is a specialized type of therapy that helps couples prepare for marriage. By participating in premarital counseling prior to their wedding, couples can begin to build a healthy, strong relationship that helps provide a healthier foundation for their union. Premarital counseling can help couples of any gender, race, or religion identify and address potential areas of conflict in their relationship. Additionally, counseling can prevent small issues from escalating into serious concerns at some point in the future.

Premarital therapy also helps couples identify their expectations for the marriage and address any significant differences they might have.

Goals and Objectives of Premarital Counseling

- Change the view of the relationship – During the therapeutic process, the counselor helps each partner examine the relationship in a more objective manner and assists the couple in learning how to perceive their interactions in a positive light.

- Understand how cultural issues affect a relationship – Family-of-origin and cultural beliefs affect how the partners understand all the relationships in their lives. It also affects day-to-day behaviors, such as eating, working, and managing money. Differences in cultural expectations can cause difficulties in the relationship. The sooner the couple learns to identify and manage these differences, the better. A counselor can help reveal these problems and teach the couple how to use the art of compromise.
- Eliminate dysfunctional behavior – Premarital counseling helps couples identify and correct dysfunctional behaviors, such as issues with dominance and control and addiction.
- Improve communication – Effective communication is one of the most important factors in a healthy relationship. In fact, as reported in "Psychology Today," psychologists believe that communication is "one of the 'three Cs' of intimacy." A premarital therapist helps couples learn how to talk to each other openly and express their thoughts and feelings in a healthy, supportive manner.
- Identify strengths – A premarital counselor can help the couple identify strengths in the relationship as a whole or in each individual partner. A thorough understanding of the stronger aspects of the union helps build resilience and a solid foundation upon which to build the marriage.
- Decrease emotional isolation and avoidance – Many people have difficulty expressing their feelings, so some partners simply avoid doing so. This type of isolation almost always leads to serious problems in the relationship. A premarital therapist assists the couple in learning how to express their feelings in a way that draws them together rather than further apart.

Common Issues Addressed in Premarital Counseling

Premarital counseling addresses a broad range of topics, including these typical issues:

- Conflict resolution – How does each partner resolve conflicts? How do their perceptions of issues correspond? How can they improve their ability to come to terms on issues on which they disagree?
- Communication – How does the couple communicate? Do they currently have an adaptive or maladaptive method for discussing important issues? How can they enhance their ability to communicate?
- Define marital expectations and beliefs – What does each partner expect from the relationship? People sometimes enter relationships with different expectations as to what constitutes a successful marriage. They often are unaware that their expectations differ until they are already married, which can lead to serious issues. A premarital therapist encourages each partner to discuss their expectations, after which the couple can work toward finding ways to compromise.
- Personal values – Do the partners have similar personal values? Research demonstrates that shared values are more important than common interests, and couples with the same values have a better chance of staying together.
- Finances – Can the couple talk about financial issues? Many people are uncomfortable

when discussing their personal finances, and issues with spending and budgeting often create conflicts in marriages. The counselor helps each partner determine his or her own financial style and then works with the couple in resolving these issues.

- Family – Do both partners want to have children? If so, how many children does each person want? For each partner, what is the optimal time to begin a family?
- Sex and intimacy – Are both partners equally comfortable — or uncomfortable — when discussing sex? What does each partner expect in terms of intimacy and a sexual relationship? Couples should speak honestly and openly about sex, even if they have chosen to remain celibate until marriage. An ability to discuss these issues without reservations helps lead to a successful marriage.

Benefits of Premarital Counseling

The many advantages of premarital therapy include:

- Helps build and strengthen conflict resolution skills – Conflict resolution skills are critical for a healthy marriage. Premarital therapy offers couples a way to identify potential conflicts and how to develop the skills necessary to get through tough battles.
- Identifies issues early – Different expectations have a disastrous effect on most marriages. Marriage therapy assists couples in determining and discussing their expectations early on. If the couple has different expectations, then the counselor can work with them to identify ways to cope with those differences.
- Helps couples avoid toxic resentment – When couples believe they are no longer in love, it's usually simply that they have allowed resentment to build up in the relationship. Resentment is toxic to happiness, and during premarital therapy, couples learn ways to avoid this type of emotional poison.
- Reduces fears about the longevity of the marriage – Statistical evidence proves that marriages end every day, which is concerning to a couple contemplating the prospect. Premarital therapy helps the couple identify and confront fears about forming and maintaining a successful relationship.

Ethical and Legal Considerations in Premarital Counseling

For counselors, premarital therapy poses both ethical and legal considerations. Some issues to consider include:

Understanding the Scope of Practice & Responsibility

Premarital therapists must understand the scope of their responsibilities and conduct premarital therapy sessions accordingly. Therapists should not provide professional services that are beyond their field of expertise based on education, experience, or lack thereof. A counselor providing premarital therapy should have specific knowledge and expertise in this specific form of treatment.

Confidentiality

Adherence to privacy is important in therapy: It allows couples and individuals an opportunity to confide in their therapist. Premarital therapists are bound by law to protect their clients' privacy, which can be difficult in actual practice. However, the therapist should explain the couple's right to confidentiality at the outset of treatment.

Patient Privilege

Therapists are obligated to protect their client's information even when called upon to testify in legal proceedings. However, counselors must disclose some specific information, no matter how private, to the authorities, including when they believe that clients might harm themselves or others. The counselor should clearly explain the concept of patient privilege during the couple's initial session.

Couples Counseling Techniques

Insight-gaining Therapy

The couples, who have arguments frequently, strain their relationship to a point that they are not able to view their problems clearly. They perpetually stay angry at each and their resentment keeps growing. After a point of time their fights become absolutely pointless and all they accomplish by that is, blaming and pointing fingers at each other.

Such couples should seek a marriage counselor that uses insight gaining therapy. In this method, the counselor studies the couple's interaction, their lifestyle and their relationship objectively. The counselor collects data about what goes on between the couple and tries to identify the root cause, the primary reason of their conflict. Then, creates a plan about how to counsel them, how to solve their problem and how to improve their way of interaction.

Communication Counseling

Communication problem is one of the major reasons why couples drift apart. There are couples who do not communicate their feelings truly due to the fear of being ridiculed or making their partner angry or unhappy. Although this does not cause any verbal conflicts or fights, it does create emotional distance between the couple.

Communication-focused-counselors are most suitable for such couples. They teach couples why expressing their feelings to their partners is crucial for their relationship and how to correctly express themselves, so that they don't hurt, annoy or infuriate their partner. They help to revamp the couple's system of interaction and fill the emotional void of their relationship.

Attachment Therapy

Couples who have been married for a long period time often experience loss of romance and passion in their relationship. The emotional distance between the couples sometimes grows to the extent that they become hesitant about sharing their personal feelings. They fear that their intimate feelings will not be validated or will be rejected by their partners, they feel ridiculous in admitting those feelings and hence they don't.

In such case attachment therapy can be useful in getting the partners closer to each other. This therapy encourages partners to speak to each other about extremely private feelings, even things that are trivial and don't really matter. This exchange of emotions helps to rejuvenate romance in the relationship and strengthens the communication between the couple.

Psychodynamic Couples Counseling

When one or both partners act somewhat irrationally in a relationship, conflicts are bound to happen. Reason behind irrational or dysfunctional behaviour can be an unpleasant childhood experience or some minor psychological disorder. Such people have distorted views about their relationship and are hence incapable of reacting rationally all the time.

A psychodynamic counselor can help such people by identifying their behavioural pattern and deciphering the reason behind the odd behaviour and counseling the affected person and their partner about rectifying that and having a better marriage.

Positive Psychology Couples Therapy

In a long term relationship the thrill and excitement sometimes gets withered and couples forget how fortunate they are to have a caring and stable partner. Positive psychology therapy helps couples to remember, acknowledge and embrace the good things that happen in their relationship everyday. In this therapy the counselor makes the couple make note of the things that made them smile and feel happy in a day. This makes couples feel positive and brings back some excitement in their relationship.

How to use Gottman Method Couples Therapy

The Gottman Method is an approach to couples therapy that includes a thorough assessment of the couple relationship and integrates research-based interventions based on the Sound Relationship House Theory.

Couples who enter into Gottman Method Couples Therapy begin with an assessment process that then informs the therapeutic framework and intervention.

Assessment

A conjoint session, followed by individual interviews with each partner are conducted. Couples complete questionnaires and then receive detailed feedback on their relationship.

Therapeutic Framework

The couple and therapist decide on the frequency and duration of the sessions.

Therapeutic Interventions

Interventions are designed to help couples strengthen their relationships in three primary areas: friendship, conflict management, and creation of shared meaning. Couples learn to replace negative conflict patterns with positive interactions and to repair past hurts. Interventions designed to increase closeness and intimacy are used to improve friendship, deepen emotional connection, and create changes which enhances the couples shared goals. Relapse prevention is also addressed.

Divorce Therapy

Divorce therapy is a form of therapy that addresses the legal, financial, and familial aspects of crumbling marriage. Divorce therapy addresses issues like: whether or not a couple should seek a separation/divorce, or try to save the marriage. If the couple decides to work on their marriage, a divorce therapist helps it set healthier, new boundaries that aid in the repair of the relationship. Divorce therapy typically occurs in a safe, non-judgmental, private counseling office.

It is considered a highly confidential form of couple's mediation. This type of therapy typically focuses on the following areas: exploring options (i.e. separation, divorce, or saving the marriage), making life changes (i.e. self-improvement, boundaries, forgiveness, patience, tolerance, etc.), indecision (i.e. not knowing what one or both spouses really want to do), trust (i.e. whether or not one or both spouses can truly forgive each other), reconciliation (i.e. repairing the damage incurred throughout the marriage), the inclusion of family (i.e. parents, in-laws, and children), and the end of the marriage (i.e. divorce and moving on).

At its best, divorce therapy helps marital couples determine what comes next – the legal and practical issues of a separation and divorce. It also helps the couple determine, if the marriage is truly worth saving. If the marriage is worth saving, a divorce therapist can provide resources to the couple to help it "get back on track." It is important to note that the end goal is not always to end the marriage; in fact, many times the ultimate goal is to save the marriage, if possible. Divorce therapy is a safe place to start an honest dialogue between the spouses, as to whether or not they want to continue in the marriage. Although, divorce therapy sounds like a last case scenario, in reality it just may be the first step to repairing a damaged marriage.

Role of a Divorce Therapist

Divorce therapists usually work with individuals after the completion of a divorce. In this capacity, the job of the divorce therapist is to help the individual come to an understanding of what went wrong and why. Working through feelings of sadness, guilt, and anger is common. Devising strategies for moving on with life is common as well. In this capacity, divorce therapists focus on solutions, working with clients to develop knowledge and skills that improve their capacity to live a happy life once again.

Divorce therapists will sometimes work with couples and families as well. In this instance, therapists may work to help prevent a divorce, or they might seek to help families cope with the aftermath of a divorce. The job here typically involves helping family members build skills that allow them to function at the highest possible level. This might include teaching ex-spouses how to communicate effectively, or working with children to develop coping strategies for living in two separate households.

Sometimes divorce therapists might assess and evaluate clients for the presence of mental health disorders, emotional difficulties, behavioral issues, or other problems that led to unhappiness in the marriage or which result from a recent divorce. Divorce therapists usually take a systems approach to understanding the problem, that is, they examine the role of each spouse as well as children, if any are present, in the dynamics of the family.

How to Help Divorcees

Divorce therapy can help a divorcee work through their divorce issues, using tried-and-true psychological methods. A divorce therapist can provide a divorcee with a trained and objective perspective for navigating the choppy waters of a separation.

One common technique is transactional analysis, which involves a set of practical conceptual tools designed to promote personal growth and change. It can help couples examine their methods of communication and choose better strategies for progressing through the divorce.

Divorce therapists can aid the divorcees with other issues, like financial obligations, living arrangements and parenting responsibilities. Therapy sessions can also aid divorcees in dealing with some of the psychological issues that contributed to the failure of their marriage, a process that can help prevent difficulties in future marriages. A divorce therapist can also counsel any children who might be involved in the divorce, easing the strain the divorce might have on these children.

A divorce therapist can also help a married couple during their divorce by acting as a mediator and guide for both parties through the divorce process. This can help minimize the feelings of hostility the couple might be feeling toward each other. During this process, couples who are constructively working together toward a divorce sometimes suddenly realize that their differences are being resolved, and they sometimes wind up cancelling the divorce and getting back together.

Work of a Divorce Therapist

Divorce therapists typically work in a clinical setting, either as part of the staff at a mental health center or in private practice. Work is usually conducted in an office setting, although on some occasions divorce therapists may visit clients' homes to evaluate the couple's or family's functioning in a more natural environment.

Divorce therapists that have a lot of experience may also work in higher education, teaching therapists-in-training about the processes and skills involved in divorce therapy. In this capacity, therapists would serve as educators in a classroom setting. Many divorce therapists offer their expertise in court proceedings as well. In this case, the therapist would work in a courtroom, offering his or her assessment of each spouse's functioning, their suitability as a parent, and their mental and emotional stability.

How to Become a Divorce Therapist

Education

As with all mental health-related professions, divorce therapists must begin with undergraduate studies in psychology, sociology, social work, or another closely related field. These programs all focus on helping students develop a general understanding of the principles of human behavior, which serve as the basis for more advanced knowledge acquisition in graduate school.

Once undergraduate studies are complete, graduate studies can commence. For individuals interested in working as a divorce therapist, a graduate program in marriage and family therapy is likely the best option, although some divorce therapists have a graduate degree in social work or another similar field. Regardless of the specific program of study, graduate students focus on developing the personal and professional skills that will allow them to provide therapy to couples that are considering divorce or have already been divorced. In addition to studying psychological theory, ethics, and statistics, graduate programs incorporate a significant practice requirement. As such, students must put what they learn into action in both simulated therapy sessions, usually with classmates, and in real-life settings with actual clients during practicum and internship experiences. Most graduate programs last 2-3 years, including these practicum and internship placements.

Individuals that choose to pursue a doctorate may do so although it is not currently required to have a doctorate to obtain licensure. Doctoral programs typically last 3-5 years, with intensive study and supervised practice in a specialized area. For example, a divorce therapist may choose to focus his or her training on working with children of divorce, or he or she may focus instead on working exclusively with couples.

Licensing Requirements

Licensure to practice divorce therapy is usually obtained as a licensed marriage and family therapist. While each state has slightly different licensure requirements, for the most part they align with the expectations of the American Association of Marriage and Family Therapists (AAMFT). AAMFT requires potential licensees have at least a master's degree from an accredited institution with two years of post-graduate clinical experience under the direction of a supervisor.

Most states also require potential therapists to pass a state licensing exam or the national licensing exam administered by AAMFT. When seeking licensure, it is best to contact the licensing body in your state of practice to determine your state's specific requirements.

Skills and Qualities Required for Becoming a Divorce Therapist

Because divorce can be an extremely traumatic situation for couples and families, divorce therapists must be able to empathize with their clients in a highly compassionate manner. They must be comforting and understanding as well, yet also challenge clients who are stuck in patterns of negative thinking. Additionally, divorce therapists must have:

- Excellent listening skills in order to give their undivided attention to clients.
- Outstanding speaking skills to discuss clients' personal issues in a professional and helpful manner.
- Exceptional interpersonal skills, and be able to work with clients from all types of backgrounds.
- Refined organizational skills, which allow them to take detailed case notes, remember minute details about a client's life, and take care of practical tasks such as billing and payments.

Job Outlook for Divorce Therapists

The job outlook for marriage and family therapists is very strong, predicted by the Bureau of Labor Statistics to be 31% over the next decade. Since marriage and family therapists are the professionals most likely to assist couples and families in divorce situations, the need for their expertise will continue to be strong as the divorce rate in the U.S. remains high. An additional factor improving the long-term outlook for practitioners that specialize in divorce therapy is that mental health services are now covered for a greater number of people after the passage of the Affordable Care Act.

Family Planning Counseling

Family planning is about deciding how many children you choose to have and when you want to have them (timing of pregnancies and birth spacing). The recommended interval before attempting the next pregnancy is at least 24 months in order to reduce risks to the mother and infant. A woman can become pregnant within several weeks after birth if she has sexual relations and if she is not breastfeeding exclusively. It is important that as a health worker you discuss the importance of family planning and birth spacing, and help couples in choosing the contraceptive method that is right for them.

The role of family planning counseling is to support a woman and her partner in choosing the method of family planning that best suits them and to support them in solving any problems that may arise with the selected method. During late pregnancy, after giving birth and after an abortion, it is important that the woman or the couple receives and discusses correct and appropriate information so that they can choose a method which best meets their needs. If a woman, preferably with her partner, is able to make an informed choice, she is more likely to be satisfied with the method chosen and continue its use.

The Health Benefits of Birth Spacing and Family Planning

- Delaying having children can give people the opportunity to complete education or further studies
- Waiting to become pregnant at least 24 months after birth can lead to health benefits for the mother and baby.

- Spacing births allows the mother to recover physically and emotionally before she gets pregnant again, and faces the demands of pregnancy, birth and breastfeeding.
- Limiting the number of children in a family means more resources for each child and more time for the parents to dedicate to each child.
- Family planning can also help couples in a sexual relationship not to be worried about the woman getting pregnant.
- STIs including HIV/AIDS can also be prevented with correct and consistent use of condoms.
- Younger women (adolescents) can delay pregnancy until their bodies are mature and they are ready in terms of their life course.
- Older women (over 35) can prevent unwanted pregnancies that are often risky for their health and can lead to complications for both mothers and infants.

When to Counsel on Birth Spacing

You should begin discussing family planning during pregnancy, particularly during the third trimester, after birth and in the immediate postpartum period. Pregnant women need to know that if they are not exclusively breastfeeding they can get pregnant as soon as four weeks after the birth of their baby, even if they have not yet started their menstrual cycle. Several methods of family planning can be started immediately after birth, but others may need to be delayed if the woman is breastfeeding.

If the woman wants female sterilization or an Intrauterine Device (IUD) inserted immediately after childbirth, she should inform her birth attendant and plan to give birth in a health facility.

Advise women about the benefits of using breastfeeding as a family planning choice, known as the Lactational Amenorrhoea Method (LAM). LAM provides protection when the following three requirements are met:

1. The woman is exclusively breastfeeding a baby, day and night
2. During the first six months after birth and
3. Her menstrual periods have not returned.

Reminder

Exclusive breastfeeding means that the baby is not given any other food or drink, not even water. She or he is only given breast milk.

Once the baby reaches six months, or receives complementary foods or the mothers' periods have returned, she should use another family planning method. Before this time she needs to start thinking about what method she will use after LAM.

Counseling a Woman on Family Planning after an Abortion

When advising a woman how to care for herself after an abortion, remember that it is important to discuss the use of a family planning method to prevent another unwanted pregnancy. Explain that she can become pregnant as soon as two weeks after an abortion if she begins to have sexual relations. A woman who has recently experienced an induced or spontaneous abortion should wait at least six months before another pregnancy to reduce risks to her health and to her future baby.

You can support her and her partner in choosing a method that meets their needs:

- If she has no post-abortion complications or infection, she can safely use any family planning method, and can start all methods immediately post-abortion (except for the natural calendar method, when she should wait for 3 months).
- If an infection is present or suspected, advise her to avoid intercourse until the infection is ruled out or fully treated. Delay female sterilization and IUD insertion until an infection is fully treated, but offer other methods to use in the meantime.
- For IUD insertion or female sterilization after a second trimester abortion, the provider may need special training because of the changed uterine size and the position of the fallopian tubes.
- If she thinks she could be at risk of getting STI/HIV, she should use a condom in all sexual relations.
- It may also be helpful to explain emergency contraception, and offer her emergency contraceptive pills to take home in case she needs them.

Male Partner

The partner should be encouraged to take part in family planning counseling sessions, especially if the chosen method involves his cooperation, for example, condoms or natural methods. In some places research has shown that family planning method use is more successful when partners choose and agree upon a method together. First, ask the woman whether she would be happy for her partner to be involved. In some cases women may feel more comfortable if their partners are not present or if their partners are counselled on their own and/or by a male Counselor.

Within the community, men also need to participate in discussions on the importance and benefits of family planning and birth spacing. Men need to understand their role in reproduction so that they can share the responsibility for family planning and birth spacing. This can be done through outreach work or through discussion with men when they accompany their wives or partners to the health facility.

Partners should be encouraged to take part in family planning counseling sessions

Women with Special Needs

Women with special needs may require extra time for family planning counseling. For example, adolescents who are not in a stable relationship, need emphasis placed on the importance of dual protection from STIs/HIV, as well as from pregnancy. They may also need special assistance in obtaining the family planning method that suits them best. Women who are in violent relationships may also need special counseling and support to explore their alternatives (i.e. condom use may be unlikely). These women may also not be able to discuss family planning with their partners and may need extra help and support in using family planning methods. Women with physical disabilities may have special requirements in terms of which methods are suitable for their situation and disability. Women with severe physical or mental disabilities may have become pregnant due to rape or abuse. The family needs to be involved in such instances to ensure that this does not recur and also possibly to be involved in discussions around family planning for this woman. Women with HIV must be counselled on the necessity of using dual protection methods, even if their partner is HIV-positive, to prevent other STIs and strains of HIV developing.

Reminder

Adolescents or unmarried women should also be offered family planning counseling. Sometimes this is difficult if the family or community disapproves of adolescent sexual activity and pregnancy. Explore ways you can work with adolescents, youth groups and schools to reach adolescents who may need support. Consider the counseling context, specifically any cultural norms you identified to help you locate any key gatekeepers in the community to help you address this topic with adolescents.

When working with a pregnant adolescent, it is particularly important to discuss birth spacing and support her in planning when she would be ready for a next pregnancy.

How to Help a Woman to Choose a Method that is Right for her

There is no single method of family planning which should be recommended for everyone. Family planning counseling can help a woman, and/or her partner choose which method best suits him or her.

There are various models of family planning counseling that can be applied, including the GATHER model (Greet the client, Ask about situation and needs, Tell about different methods and options, Help clients choose, Explain how to use a method, Return) or the REDI model (Rapport-building, Exploration, Decision-making, and Implementing the decision). In general, the steps or actions outlined below should be covered to counsel on family planning.

1. Assess the Situation, her Needs and Information Gaps

In order to help counsel a woman on family planning, it is very important to discuss her and her partner's specific needs and situation.

1. You can ask if she knows about family planning, what she has heard about it, and if she knows it is important;
2. Explain that it is important to know that she can become pregnant soon after giving birth if she is not exclusively breastfeeding;
3. You should also ask whether the woman or couple already have a family planning method in mind – those people who receive the method that they have planned for are much more likely to use it successfully. You can then help them assess if this method suits their situation and needs (e.g., Are you confident you could remember to take a pill every day?), or it may also be helpful to discuss other options in case there is a method that better suits his/her or their needs.

When discussing her needs and situation, you can ask about:

- Plans for having more children;
- Whether she and/or her partner want to use family planning;
- Previous methods used and reasons for success or failure;
- Experience with side-effects;
- Popular beliefs about family planning and how these affect her decision to choose a particular method;
- Her relationship and situation; Is she in a stable relationship? How often does she see her partner? How many partners does she have?; Is there need for dual protection from STIs, including HIV?
- Her and her partner's HIV status or risk factors for HIV;
- Regularity of sexual intercourse (especially for adolescents or unmarried women);
- Partner's or family's views about family planning methods;
- Ability to keep to routines.

2. Help to prioritize solutions, narrow down options and make a good choice

You can then discuss various family planning methods based on the needs and situation of the woman and her partner. Key method characteristics that can be discussed include:

- Can the method be used while breastfeeding?
- How effective is it?
- Are there any side-effects?

- Does it provide protection from STIs or HIV?
- Does it impact on sexual relations?
- How easy is it to use?
- Is it easy to stop using the method?
- Is the method reversible?
- How quickly will fertility return once method is stopped?
- Is there a need to do something before sex? (e.g. putting a condom on, inserting a diaphragm)
- Is it used continuously, or only used when needed?
- Is there a need to touch genitals?

3. Check if she is eligible to use the chosen method

Before giving out detailed information on method use, check if the woman is eligible to use the method. Some women who have recently given birth or who are breastfeeding may be unable to use certain methods. You can also check if she is able to start using the family planning method straight away. Some health conditions may prevent a woman from using certain methods.

4. Provide useful information on the chosen method

Women and their partners need accurate information to use a family planning method correctly. Although too much information can be unhelpful or off-putting, there are some key pieces of information that must be explained:

- What the method is and how it works
- How effective it is at preventing pregnancy
- Side-effects: what the user can expect, and what to do about them
- How to use the method correctly
- What to do in case of a mistake in the use of the method or problems (missed pills, late for injection, condom splits)
- Information on when to return to the clinic
- Signs of complications to watch out for.

The best way to check whether a woman knows how to use the method is to ask her to explain to you in her own words how to use the method. You could also ask her to demonstrate the use of certain methods such as condoms or diaphragms, or you could consider demonstrating their use to her first, asking for her to repeat back the demonstration afterwards to ensure that she has fully understood.

Child Adoption and Behavioral Counseling

5

Families need support before and after adoption in the form of pre-adoption and post-adoption counseling which allow parents to understand the emotional and behavioral needs of an adopted child. Behavior counseling is focused at changing behaviors of a concerned individual through therapy such as dealing with anger management issues, suicidal tendencies, depression, etc. This chapter explores some of the fundamental aspects of child adoption and behavioral counseling and includes the ways to tackle simple and complex issues faced by clients in these domains.

Adoption Counseling

Adoption counseling, sometimes also called pregnancy counseling, is designed to help expectant mothers explore their options and learn more about the possibility of adoption. These services are available to every potential birth mother, free of charge and with no obligation to continue with an adoption plan.

Adoption counseling offers a number of benefits to women at every stage of the adoption process, from the initial request for adoption information through delivery and post-placement support. Your adoption counselor will provide the support and guidance you need every step of the way.

Why should I Seek Adoption Counseling

You are facing one of the most difficult decisions a woman can make. You may be wondering where to turn for help or worrying whether you are making the right choice. Alternatively, you might feel confident in your adoption decision and feel ready to begin the process.

Either way, adoption counseling services are highly recommended. However you are feeling about your adoption options, adoption counseling offers significant practical and emotional benefits. Here are just a few reasons to consider contacting an adoption counselor:

- You can learn more about all of your options, not just adoption. Adoption counselors do not want to match pregnant women with adoptive families if they are not certain that the adoption will be successful. This means that your counselor will help you evaluate all of your options, as well as your own wants and needs, to determine whether adoption is truly the best choice for you.
- You will have help navigating the adoption process. If you do choose to proceed with an adoption plan, your counselor or social worker can help you make important decisions for your baby throughout the process and coordinate the services you need. They will be with you every step of the way as you create your adoption plan, find an adoptive family, and go through the legal process of placing your baby for adoption.
- You will have an advocate who understands your individual needs. Adoption counselors have worked with many birth mothers from all different backgrounds, and they know that every woman needs varying types and amounts of emotional support. Your counselor can provide individualized support based on your unique needs.

- You will be able to process difficult feelings in your own way. Every prospective birth mother experiences moments of doubt, pain and grief. Your adoption counselor can help you understand these feelings and, when you are ready, heal in a healthy way.
- You will have guidance as you build a relationship with the adoptive family. Whether you want an open, semi-open or closed adoption, your counselor can help you build the relationship you want to have with the adoptive family. She can facilitate contact, help you get to know each other, and keep you in contact with your child for years to come.
- You may receive help addressing additional needs or concerns. Women who choose adoption have many different reasons for doing so. If you are considering adoption because of an underlying issue, such as a lack of familial support, financial or housing instability, an abusive relationship or substance abuse, your counselor can help you find additional resources to help address some of these problems.
- You can remain anonymous until you are ready to make an adoption plan. If you want more information about your adoption options, you can contact an adoption counselor to request this information without providing identifying information.
- You are always in control of your adoption plan. You can talk with your counselor regularly through every step of the process, or only check in occasionally as you need support. You can also change or discontinue your adoption plan at any time. It's up to you to decide exactly what services you need, what type of adoption experience you want to have, and what type of relationship you want to have with your adoption counselor.

How to Become Adoption Counselor

Adoption counselors work with parents who are considering and completing adoption. They are sometimes referred to as adoption consultants, adoption social workers or adoption advocates. An adoption counselor can work with people who may be giving up a child, as well as those who are looking to adopt. Adoption counseling requires experience in social work or psychology. You should be able to aid parents through successful or unsuccessful adoption processes, providing emotional counseling, parenting instruction, child transfer and adoption problem-solving. You will need to have exceptional patience, communication skills and desire to help people through an exciting but difficult time.

Steps

1. Earn a bachelor's degree in counseling, psychology, public health or social work. You will be

working directly with clients, so you should be highly trained on how to work through conflict, provide emotional support and work with government or other agencies.

2. Apply for an internship with a counseling office or agency. Take this opportunity to gain experience working with people who are going through an emotional process. Also, decide whether you have the communication skills and emotional strength to handle the requirements of the job.

3. Decide how you would like to work as an adoption counselor. You may choose who you want to help in the adoption process, which can affect where you work.

- Apply for work in a family planning clinic. You can counsel young mothers and fathers about choosing to give their child up for adoption. If you have an interest in health care or working with teenagers, this may be the best option for you.
- Apply for work in a government agency. If you want to work in public health, you can become an adoption counselor for Health and Human Services, or a similar agency. You can help foster children to become adopted and work with older children who are seeking adoption.
- Apply for work with a private adoption organization. You may want to work with adoptions originating outside of the United States. In this case, you will need to gain expertise on cultural adoption issues and vetting processes of your employer.
- Apply for work as a group adoption counselor. You can provide counseling that addresses the emotional hardships of the adoption process, such as failure to conceive or long waiting periods. People who have achieved higher degrees in counseling or psychology will be well suited to support groups through private or public employers.

4. Apply for your state license as a counselor, family therapist or clinical social worker. Contact your state licensing board to inquire whether this is required in your area. If you move to a new state, you may be required to apply for a new license.

5. Apply for an entry-level position in an adoption agency. You can apply to government agencies, family services agencies and private adoption agencies. You may be required to assist colleagues before you take your own cases.

6. Consider a master's degree in social work, counseling or psychology. If you want to move into management roles in an adoption office, you will need to have the clinical practice and training you get with a graduate degree. Most people in these programs can specialize, so you can focus on adoption counseling.

How to do Adoption Counseling

It is very common for families to need support before and after adoption. Pre and post adoption services can help families with a wide range of issues. Experience with past adoptive families has shown that all family members can benefit from receiving some type of pre and post-adoption support.

Pre-Adoption Counseling

Entering into the adoption process can be frightening, and some people feel they need a sense of balance and certainty. Counseling can help. In addition, sometimes families have issues that must be resolved before the integration of a child, who may have emotional and behavioral needs that could be challenging for even the most stable family. This counseling can help you focus on your specific needs, such as family-of-origin issues or having experienced abuse.

These needs can be met through: Educational Workshops, Support Groups, and Family Counseling Services

Post-Adoption Counseling

Loss and Grief: Even when children have a positive adoption experience, they often feel some level of separation and loss or possibly even abandonment. They may need support in working through their feelings, mourning their losses, and accepting who they are.

Trust and Attachment Related Issues : Children who have experiences abuse, neglect, out-of-home care or institutionalization often have difficulty trusting and attaching to their adoptive family. They may need assistance in building these relationships.

Identity Formation: "Who am I? How am I different from my parents? How am I like my birth parents?" Helping children understand who they are for themselves in their own person.

Family Dynamics and Adoption Adjustment: Adoptive parents sometimes experience loss and grief, maybe about infertility, maybe because the adoption is not going as they expected, all of which can cause a strain to a marriage and/or the family. Counseling may help the individual and the family.

Connection to the Birth Family: Some need help working through their feelings surrounding their birth parents and why they were placed for adoption and some may need help navigating how to search for their birth family. A counselor could assist in these situations.

Difficulties that children who were in out-of-home care before adoption experience: Maybe a child has effects of early trauma in their lives, maybe they have health issues, school issues, trans-cultural issues, etc. A counselor may be able to assist the child and the parents in navigating through these issues.

Depression and Anxiety: Many adoptive parents suffer from post-placement blues and anxiety from the money, time, effort, emotional strain, and patience needed throughout the adoption journey. Counselors can help with adjustment and provide assistance with coping strategies.

Stress Management: Stress can be caused by the addition of a new family member, lack of sleep, increased family responsibilities, and increased financial responsibilities among many other things. A counselor can assist with managing stressful situations.

Behavioral/Emotional Difficulties: Some adopted children may develop emotional and behavioral issues. The problems may or may not result from insecurities or issues related to being adopted.

Developmental/Learning Concerns: Delays can be caused by genetic or environmental factors (including exposure to alcohol or other drugs during pregnancy, trauma, neglect, or insecure attachment). Children learn and develop at different rates, so some children may be slightly behind their peers. With international adoptions, learning a second language or adjusting to a new culture may also create temporary delays. A counselor can help with understanding your concerns and can refer families to additional resources if necessary.

Trauma, Abuse, or Neglect: Adopted children who have experienced trauma, abuse, or neglect in their lifetime can lack trust in others and have a heightened sensitivity to certain situations. It is important for adoptive families to make the home a structures, safe, and nurturing environment. A counselor can assist with issues or concerns surrounding abuse, trauma, and neglect.

Sibling Issues and Attachment: Counselors can help families work through issues regarding sibling acceptance and attachment with adopted children.

Nutritional, Eating, and Sleep Issues: Often children who have come from foster homes or orphanages have special nutritional needs as well as issues with food. Meals are at least a three-times a day event, so the relationship your child has with food can often affect your child's attachment with you as well as their overall physical growth and health. Many families need help with food-related issues.

Sleep is also an everyday event, and parents can often become exacerbated when their child has difficulty sleeping. We can help provide you with some practical tips as well as determine if there may be more serious issues at hand.

Other Post-Adoption Counseling: Older Child Issues, Adjustment to New Parenting Roles, Marital Difficulties and more.

How to Guide Clients to be Good Parents

The counselors can guide their clients by providing the parenting tips to the first timers.

1. Identify your child's strengths. You can use them to build your child's self-esteem, helping to provide the confidence he or she needs to tackle whatever seems difficult. Children will be more willing to listen and understand how to correct adverse behaviors if their dignity is intact.

2. Punishing a child is not as effective as using praise and rewards. Rather than focusing on weaknesses, find ways to assist your child in developing to his or her full potential. When encouraged, children will acquire talents to compensate for any deficiencies.

3. Avoid negative emotional reactions, such as anger, sarcasm, and ridicule. If your child has problems with control, negativity will only make him or her feel worse. Use short and mild suggestions to remind your child to focus, like "P.A.," for "pay attention."

4. Don't compare siblings. If a child thinks his or her brother or sister is favored, it can create a rivalry that may last the rest of their lives and cause problems in your family. Make sure your kids know that they are loved equally.

5. Get support if you need it. Life with children is a roller coaster ride. Understanding that there will be negative aspects to child rearing and getting some professional advice when necessary will help you maintain your sanity and enjoy the experience.

6. Children need positive attention. If they do not receive positive attention from family, they may choose to seek out negative attention. This is because negative attention is still attention, and any attention is better than being ignored. Remember to communicate with your child. Love and care are the greatest healers.

7. Monitor your child's use of the Internet. The stuff kids can access in cyberspace can be dangerous. Get a program that will let you see the web sites they visit and monitor their chats.

8. Accept that life changes when you have a child. Lazy Saturday mornings in bed are replaced by soccer games and recitals. Remember, you still need to make time for each other – date nights and weekend getaways are important for your relationship.

9. Parent by example. Think of your kids as little bipedal copy machines who will mimic everything you do. If you behave badly, you are giving them permission to act in the same ways. Check in with yourself, and don't lose it in front of the children.

10. Don't give up on your child, ever. All of your child's problems can be worked through with humor, goodwill, and perseverance. With proper parental support, even the most troublesome teens can become amazing people.

How to Guide Clients Parenting Tips to Parents of Preschoolers

The adoption counselors can guide the adopting parents by giving them tips to parent their new preschoolers.

1. Polishing their Communication Skills

Communication skills of toddlers are equally important. Clearer their communication skills are, better they will fare with other kids and teachers once they start commuting to a preschool.

2. Teach her to be a Good Listener

We all know that it's challenging to contain the capricious mind of a toddler. However, at preschool she will have to take part in various activities such as singing, drawing, listening to her teacher's explanation and so on. All these will require her to sit still and pay attention. Being a good listener will help her proactively take part in various activities at her preschool.

3. Encourage Teamwork

Again, apart from spending time at home, she will be spending a good 4-5 hours with other kids and teachers at her preschool, taking part in various group activities. These activities require teamwork, and you can encourage this skill in her by playing games with her at home.

4. Teach her to Follow Instructions

At a young age, we learn through instructions and directions given to us. However, it won't go that easy, if you don't know how to follow directions. In preschool, your child will take directions from her teacher to take part in various fun activities. Guide her how to follow instructions by playing games with her, give her fun tasks and take part in it with her.

5. Helping her to Work with Stationery

Preschools offer various activities which require the use of objects such as pencil, crayon, scissors, wax or colour pencils. You can help her how to handle them correctly by encouraging her to draw and write more. You can teach her writing strokes of alphabets, numbers, etc.

6. Encourage her to be Independent

At home, you are there to wipe and clean her after various activities such as eating or playing. You are there to help her to wash her hands before and after her meal. However, while in preschool you can't be there with her. Encourage her to be independent so she can wipe her mouth or nose, or wash her hands on her own. It also generates a sense of responsibility and independence in them, which will be helpful for them in the coming years.

7. Have a Set Routine

Having a set routine for various activities such as playing, meal, snack, sleep, etc., is important for both of you. Not only it will teach discipline to your kid, but it will also help you manage your own time efficiently. Another advantage is that you won't have to run after them each time to remind them to have their meals on time or to put them to bed.

8. Try not to be Too Strict

Discipline should not be confused with strictness. Children tend to be stubborn if you are too strict with them. Instead talk to them in a friendly manner, win their trust so they can communicate to you without fear. It will also help you to have a strong bond with them.

9. Don't Give in to Their Tantrums

Having said that, you can't be too mellow as well. Try to find the right balance that is neither too strict nor too soft. Don't put a blind eye to your child's tantrums, instead, direct them to do something else if they are throwing their tantrum over something. The best way is to identify the cause of their such behaviour. Is it due to hunger or sleep, or are they tired?

10. Don't Treat them Like an Adult

Many parents expect way too much out of their children. Try to understand that they are still at a delicate learning stage, and, they are still kids. Don't expect to understand everything you tell them immediately. Have patience and let them learn their own pace. The important thing is that you encourage them to learn and keep on trying. You may want to find out what interests and motivates them. Be creative when you give them tasks, and ensure that it's fun for both of you rather than a chore which you have to go through.

11. Don't be a "No" Person Always

It might be challenging, but there are ways to go about it. Try not to say, "No" very often. A kid's heart is quite sensitive, and they may feel unloved, or undesirable if you say no to them often. Moreover, it might also lead to a rebelling attitude in them. Try talking to them at their level, and nicely explain the situation if you have to say no to something.

12. Praise them for Being Good

Compliment them for their good work. It would positively encourage a child. On the other hand, if they have done something wrong then let them know why it is wrong. Such awareness will make them conscious of what they are doing and whether it will have a negative consequence.

13. Don't Put too Many Things on Her Plate

Every child is different and learns at her own pace. As a parent, of course, you will have certain expectations of her. However, it is also a job of a parent to understand their child and accept their capabilities. Don't try to put too many things on her plate at once, remember she is still a kid. Keep a balanced schedule which is comfortable for her.

14. Be a Role Model to Them

They will be spending most of their time with you. And how you behave, what you do, how you do things, etc., all of these impact on their development. Be a role model to them so they can look up to you.

15. Creating Strong Bond

Raising a kid can be challenging, but it's a learning phase for both, i.e., a parent and child. It is important that you are engaged in fun activities together. Doing things together will help you create trust and a strong bond with your child. You should be a parent as well as a friend to them whom they can rely upon without hesitation.

Child Counseling

Child counseling is a specialized area of psychology focused on working with children who have a mental illness, have experienced a traumatic event, or are facing a difficult family situation. Child counseling often deals with many of the same issues that adults do, such as anxiety or grief, but this type of therapy focuses on breaking these problems down so that children can understand and make sense of them.

Child counselors are specialists who can offer insight into the inner workings of your child's development that are not necessarily visible to even those closest to the child. Most important of all, your child may not be able to tell you what sort of help they need, so your judgment is critical in ensuring your child receives the therapeutic intervention that is best for them.

Child Counseling can help kids interpret issues in a way that they can understand.

Child counselors and therapists are highly trained in the thought processes of children so they can help kids and youths to interpret issues or trauma in a way that they can understand. When a child's emotional issues are left untreated, it's likely that they'll impact the child's educational and development and can also persist into adulthood.

Children of all ages can attend counseling sessions, from young preschoolers to teenagers. Every age within this range falls into the realm of child counseling until they are adults and no longer need children's counseling techniques.

Child counseling aims to help children work through their emotions so they can live normal healthy lives without fear, confusion, anxiety or trauma in their lives.

Types of Child Counseling

Cognitive-behavior therapy (CBT)

CBT focuses on helping children change negative styles of thinking and behaving by correcting or re-purposing the thought process toward a more positive response. CBT challenges the automatic internal beliefs a child has about themselves and teaches them to view themselves and their situation through a more realistic and positive lens. CBT provides children with practical tools for coping with difficult or stressful situations that they can learn to use on their own.

Trauma-Focused CBT (TF-CBT)

TF-CBT is designed to help children overcome the effects of trauma. As with traditional CBT, children are taught to see events more realistically without blaming themselves. TF-CBT teaches children strategies that they can use when they experience a flashback so they can work through the memories from a place of control and understanding, and gives them the ability to use these tools on their own.

Alternative Therapies

Children respond well to alternative types of therapies like art therapy, music therapy, movement therapy, equine therapy, mindfulness, or aquatic therapy.

Some of the most common issues that child counseling addresses are:

- Divorce
- Death of a loved one and grief
- Witnessing or experiencing a trauma
- Mental health diagnoses, including anxiety and depression
- Bullying
- Sexual, emotional, or physical abuse
- Relocating schools or cities
- Substance abuse or addiction in the family

Goals of Child Counseling

Child counseling addresses major issues in a child's life with the intended outcome being that they can learn tools to deal with stress or trauma. Some of the common goals of child counseling include being able to cope with difficult situations such as:

Anxiety

Children who attend counseling are encouraged to learn techniques to deal with emotional distress and anxiety on their own. Children can learn to prevent panic attacks or cope with anxiety in a variety of ways, which they will learn in their counseling sessions. Some strategies they will learn may include breathing exercises, changing negative self-talk, muscle relaxation, talking to a trusted adult about their feelings instead of keeping them inside, and asserting themselves by knowing when to remove themselves from a stressful situation. Teaching these techniques to children gives them a toolbox of coping mechanisms that they can use when they become anxious or experience a panic attack.

Trauma

Unfortunately, some children experience traumatic events and are exposed to disturbing situations that they should not have to witness or be part of. After a trauma, a child may experience shock, disbelief, detachment or emotional numbness, fear, and may develop post-traumatic stress disorder. Symptoms of PTSD include strong desire to avoid the people or places where trauma was involved, vivid and distressing memories or flashbacks, nightmares or insomnia or fear of going to sleep, and being easily angered or agitated. Child counseling aims to help children talk about the trauma that they faced, rather than keeping their experiences and emotions inside. Many children who experience trauma develop trust issues and may have a difficulty finding the words to express their feelings and may blame themselves for what happened.

Child counseling teaches children that it's okay to talk about their experiences and that they can use a variety of coping mechanisms. When a child has a flashback to their trauma, child counselors teach them tools such as deep breathing, seeking out an adult to talk to, relaxing their muscles, and correcting the misinterpretation of traumatic events.

Divorce

When a marriage dissolves, it can be very challenging for children in the family to cope with. Many children blame themselves for their parents splitting up or have feelings that they are unloved. With divorce often comes changes in custody, and in some cases, there are tense custody battles between parents. Children can feel guilty about choosing which parent they want to live with and feel distress if their choices or feelings don't align with their siblings. Child counseling teaches children to deal with feelings of sadness, fear, and guilt by giving them techniques to use such as deep breathing, journaling or art therapy, practicing positive self-talk, and talking about their feelings with their parents or another trusted adult.

Grief

A death of a loved one, whether it's a family member, peer, or friend of the family is distressing for anyone; however, children often cannot cope with death in the same way that adults can. For children, it may be difficult to understand their feelings of loss, despair, sadness, and missing the person who died. Often, children may have irrational thoughts such as the fear that they will also die, thinking that the death was their fault, or believing that they could have prevented it. Child counseling helps children understand the grieving process and teaches them that it's okay to experience the emotions that arise after losing a loved one. Coping strategies may include being able to talk about their feelings, channeling grief through creative pursuits like journaling or art, and allowing themselves to speak or think about their loved one through sharing personal memories. Teaching children the stages of grief is another technique that helps them understand that how they feel is normal and natural.

Significant Change

For many children, events, like moving to a new city or changing schools, can be stressful. Many adults can accept these changes as part of life, so you may not realize the impact it has on your child. Children who have difficulty dealing with change can experience feelings of insecurity, anxiety or worry, or anger towards their parents. While these are normal reactions to significant change, many children have a hard time moving past these feelings on their own. Child counseling teaches children to cope with change through learning to focus on the positive and stable aspects of their life, positive self-talk, deep breathing exercises when anxiety arises, and understanding that change is natural, understanding that their feelings are temporary and will fade when they adjust to the situation.

Self-Esteem and Confidence

Many children struggle with poor self-esteem and low confidence which can lead to depression, substance abuse, eating disorders, or thoughts of self-harm. When a child has poor self-esteem, they may feel unloved, worthless, and their friends and family would be better off without them. Child counseling can help children improve their self-esteem in a variety of ways, including digging deeper into underlying issues that may have caused these beliefs, recognizing negative self-talk and turning it into positive thoughts, using affirmations to gain confidence and self-acceptance, and talking to a trusted adult when troubling feelings arise. If a child's low self-esteem has developed into something more serious, like an eating disorder, child counselors are equipped to help children overcome those issues.

How to Become a Child Therapist

Children can suffer similar mental health disorders as adults, including grief, depression, anxiety, and post-traumatic stress disorder. These children need the same in-depth psychological counseling as adults. Being a child therapist, or a child counselor, can be a great way to help children overcome these mental discomforts. Your role will be to help with prevention and intervention with these children. You may work as a college instructor or professor or work in a lab. Or, you may be a practicing clinician. With any of these positions, you will be expected to focus on your education and your ability to communicate, especially with children and their families.

Method 1. Preparing for an Undergraduate Degree

1. Prepare for many years of education. To become a child psychologist, you will be expected to complete at least a Master's Degree, preferably a PhD or doctorate. The first step to this career is to prepare yourself to focus on your education.

- Make sure you have the financial means to go to school. This may involve taking out student loans.

- You can offset some of these costs by looking for scholarships. The United States offers scholarships based on good grades in high school.
- Talk to your school counselor or your preferred undergraduate school to see what financial assistance they offer. In many cases, colleges have a dedicated financial aid department to help you with this.

2. Strive for good grades in high school. In preparing to go to college, it is important to stand as a strong candidate for college. To do this, you should focus on:

- Developing good study habits to do well on tests and homework. This includes taking good notes and having a good rapport with your teachers and mentors.
- Stay on top of your homework. Homework is often an important part of your grade. Make sure you do all of your homework for each class.
- Develop good time-management strategies. This is an essential skill that will help you be effective in the real world as well as your job. Establishing a good routine in high school will help you develop good habits that will carry over to your future.

3. Learn the good, and the bad, of the job. Before you invest a lot of time and effort into education, make sure you are looking at careers realistically. A high-paying child psychologist job may seem glamorous, but be sure of the good and the not-so-good aspects about a job.

- Think about the amount of time you want to work. Do you want to work a 40 hour a week, or an 80 hour one?
- Do you want a job where you will travel or stay in one spot?

- Do you want to work with a team or alone?
- Do you think you can handle a stressful job situation where you may have to talk to children who have suffered some terrible things?
- How will you handle the stress of this career?

4. Learn appropriate skills. You should acquire skills and keep practicing them. These will most certainly help you in a future career. In fact, one of the tests you must pass in order to be a practice child psychology requires testing some of these skills. Consider the following:

- Analytical skills — learn by practicing logic puzzles and solving problems.
- Communication skills — take a speech class or practice public speaking in front of a mirror.
- Observational skills — write down an idea log which helps you reflect on what you have observed throughout the day. This has been proven to improve observational skills.
- Patience -- Remind yourself to take your time. Make this a habit.
- People skills — Try and get to know people and work well with them.
- Trustworthiness -- Try and be as honest as possible so you can be someone a patient can trust.

Method 2. Obtaining an Undergraduate Degree

1. Apply for an undergraduate degree. An undergraduate degree is a must have in child counseling. When applying to school, make sure the school has the appropriate programs. You can often

research specific programs on the school's website. You'll want to look for a school that meets the following criteria:

- It is accredited and legally able to grant a degree.
- It offers programs in clinical psychology, forensic psychology, industrial-organizational psychology, or sports psychology.

2. Take helpful classes. You will want to take the classes that will help to grant your degree. A school advisor should be able to help you make sure you are doing so. However, you should also consider taking electives or additional classes that will help you stand out as a candidate for graduate school and a career. These classes may include:

- Biology and anatomy courses
- Sociology courses
- Math and science courses
- Communication, public speaking, and writing courses
- Nursing courses
- Any psychology courses (even if they're not specialized in children. This is a great opportunity to learn more about how the brain works).

3. Cultivate connections. Since you know you will likely be going to graduate school, it is important to make connections and friends with people in the field. You will need these connections to:

- Ask for letters of recommendations.
- Have friends in the field.
- Have potential mentors to help you in the future.
- Help you get into graduate school.
- Help you obtain a job.

4. Prepare for graduate school. In your junior year of your undergraduate, you will want to start to think seriously about graduate school. This is the time where you will start to research schools and collect application materials. At this time, you should think about:

- Geographically, where you might want to attend school.
- Who you might ask for letters of recommendation.
- What written material or research you will want to submit into your application.
- If you can afford graduate school, or will you need to start to look for assistantships or scholarships.

Method 3. Pursuing a Graduate Degree

1. Research graduate programs. Before you apply to graduate school, you will need to research the type of graduate school you would like to enter. There are many schools out there, but you will want to look for a school that will help you focus on what specific career you are looking for. For example:

- If you are looking for a school you can do research, you may want to look into RI institutions, which are ranked the best for research.
- If you want to specifically work in counseling and prevention, you should consider a school that offers specific clinicals or internships.
- If you want to teach child psychology, consider entering a school with an emphasis in pedagogy and teaching.

2. Ask for letters of recommendation. You need to call on your old connections to ask if they would be willing to write you a letter of recommendation. These connections should be people that can reflect on your academic, professional, or personal merit.

- You may consider asking old professors, primary investigators (from labs), advisors, or employers (if applicable).

3. Write a statement of purpose. Many graduate schools require a statement of purpose/intent for their applications. These statements ask you to specifically articulate why you want to enter the program and what you will bring to the school.

4. Take GRE or MCAT. Some graduate schools will require you take the GRE, which is a general

graduate school examination (similar to the ACT/SAT for undergraduates). As of 2015, the MCAT, traditionally used for medical school, added psychology and sociology to their tests. Your school of choice will more than likely have a preference on which you will need to take.

- Both the GRE and the MCAT have test prep materials on their websites. Often, when you sign up for these tests, you will have an opportunity to take practice tests.

5. Apply to graduate school. After you have your materials together, it is time to apply to graduate school. This process can be daunting, but it helps immensely if you have prepared your materials in advance. Here are common requirements for graduate school applications:

- Statement of intent/purpose
- Writing sample
- Letters of recommendation (usually 3)
- High school and undergraduate transcripts
- GRE/MCAT scores
- FASFA information
- TESOL/TEFOL information (if applicable)

6. Make connections. Just like undergraduate, you will want to make connections to cohorts and mentors alike. They can really help you secure a job or help you with whatever you may struggle with. In graduate school, work can sometimes be overwhelming, take advantage of:

- Departmental meet-and-greets
- Opportunities to present research
- University programs specifically for graduate students (for example, Graduate Student Senate or a graduate student psychology group)
- Invited presentations/lectures

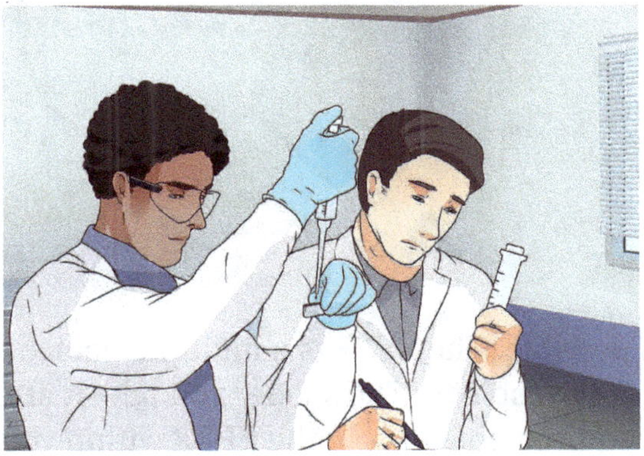

7. Start inquiring about jobs. Graduate programs should have some way to help you obtain a job when you graduate. This might be required professional development including clinical work or internships. Or, you might have an opportunity to do laboratory work with a mentor or professor.

- Always keep an eye out for these opportunities, even if they are not mandatory, as they can go a long way in helping you to secure a job.

Method 4. Obtaining Licensing

1. Decide where you wish to practice. Licensing varies state by state and, though it has become easier to obtain licensure mobility (the ability to obtain licensing in other jurisdictions), you should try to have an idea of where you'd like to practice and where you might like to practice in the future.

- Learn the current licensing laws specific to your state and other states where you would consider living. You can research the license requirements unique to each state by entering the relevant information on the ASPPB website.
- Most states will require that you have obtained your post-doctorate, pass the Examination

for Professional Practice of Psychology (EPPP), pass a jurisprudence or ethics exam, pass an an oral exam, and that you've completed a certain number or hours (between 1,500 and 6,000) of "supervised professional experience" (the definition of which varies by state).

2. Take the EPPP as soon as possible. The EPPP is a multiple-choice test that covers your foundational, text book knowledge of psychology. The sooner you take it after grad school, the less you'll have to re-learn. Check the requirements to take the EPPP within your state.

- You need to get about 70% of the questions correct to pass the EPPP. You are not penalized for incorrect answers, so if you find yourself running out of time (the test takes 4 hours and 15 minutes), it's better to guess the answers than to leave them blank.
- Take practice exams to familiarize yourself with the types of questions you will be asked and to get used to the time limitations. Go back over the test and figure out where your knowledge is strong and in which subjects you'll need to review heavily.

3. Get your supervised professional experience hours. This can be tricky, as state requirements can vary widely. On average, states require between 3,000 – 4,000 hours of experience. What qualifies as experience can also vary from state to state. Your state may or may not require internships to be APA-accredited.

- Cover your bases by fulfilling the maximum number of hours required in most states. Even if the state in which you currently live only requires 1,500 hours, you should aim for 2,000 hours in an APA-accredited internship and 2,000 hours in a supervised postdoc. This will give you the most flexibility and mobility later on, as this will fulfill most state requirements.

4. Pass your jurisprudence exam. Again, this will vary by state, so you need to research the requirements to find out when you are eligible to take the test, the topics covered, and how to get approval to take the exam. It may be online, taken in a classroom, open or closed book.

- This exam will cover state-specific laws and the ethics code of the APA.

5. Take the oral exam, if required. Depending on your state, you may also need to pass an oral exam. The purpose and format of these exams is incredibly varied, so research the requirements within your state to prepare.

Method 5. Obtaining Certifications

1. Research certifications. If you live, or intend to practice in the United States, you will be working with the American Board of Professional Psychology (ABPP) to earn certifications. You will need to have earned your license to pursue other certifications.

- It is always a good idea to talk to a trusted adviser about what examinations and certifications you should pursue. Some jobs require unique certifications, but almost all require passing the ABPP certification.

2. Prepare for credentials review. This first stage of the ABPP examination is just an objective examination of your educational history. The review board will make sure you have successfully completed the appropriate schooling necessary. This includes both your undergraduate and graduate studies and includes any accomplished research or publication.

3. Pass the practice sample review. This is the second part of the ABPP examination and requires you to pass a written examination based on the field. The organization will ask you to submit a statement of purpose detailing your content expert knowledge of your preferred field.

4. Ace your oral examinations. Depending on how well you do on the previous portions of the exams, the board may ask you to be able to orally defend your material. This is just a review of your previous supplied materials.

- Often, this is organized depending on the needs of the review board.

5. Demonstrate domains of competency. The last part of the examination is for you to show that you are competent in your expertise. The board requires you to submit evidence of successful practice. This may include a recording of you in a therapy session or evidence of laboratory work.

- This state of the examination is dependent on your future career goals. The board will help you determine what will be appropriate to submit at this portion.

Method 6. Applying for a Job

1. Recognize job growth. Luckily, the field of child psychology is a growing field of about a growth rate of 14% per year.

2. Obtain a job through clinicals/internships. You will more-than-likely have to do some sort of professional development through your schooling. This might be a great time to secure a position.

Ask your manager or your managing professor to see if you can get a full-time job through this internship.

- These professional development opportunities are another great way to make a great impression in the field. More than likely, a hiring manager may know other similar people in the field.

3. Search online.There are many psychology-specific job boards out there. Check hospitals and agencies in your area to see if they have an open position.

- Often, colleges post instructor/professor positions on their college job board. You can check your local colleges (or college website) for open positions.

4. Talk to connections. You have spent a lot of time in education.Talk to your connections that you have made in the past. Contact your professors and your classmates to see where you can get a position.

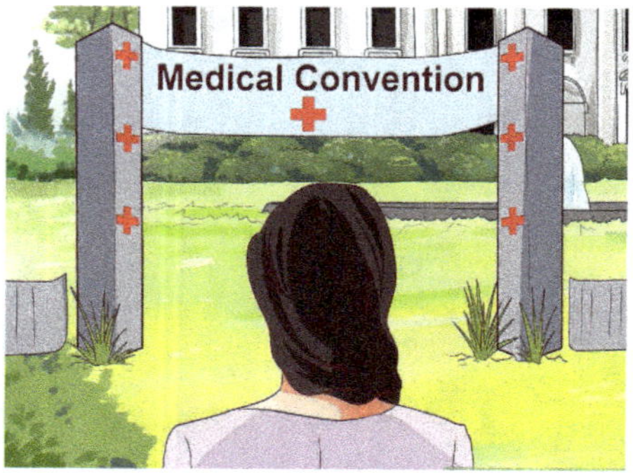

5. Go to medical conventions. Medical and psychological associations, like the American Psychology Association (APA), hold fairs for future clinicians.

How to use different Techniques for Child Counseling

Therapeutic Games

Selected games and activities help a child learn self-management strategies. For instance, a counselor may blow bubbles with a child. While the child is having fun with the bubbles, the counselor demonstrates how to blow bigger bubbles by taking deep breaths and blowing slowly. The counselor then explains how "Bubble Breaths" can help relieve anxiety. Strategy games -- such as checkers and Battleship -- help children learn impulse control by thinking about consequences. Memory games, such as card matching, help a child with Attention Deficit Hyperactivity Disorder increase his attention span and improve memory, according to "Fun and Games: Help ADHD Children Learn From Play," published by ADDitude.

Art Therapy

For diagnostic purposes, counselors may give a child an assignment, such as copying, picture completion or instructions to draw a particular thing, such as an animal or the child's family. At other times, free choice of art media and subject matter provide a child the opportunity to freely express inner thoughts and feelings. Counselors interpret a child's art by looking for themes and by asking the child to discuss his project. An unstructured approach to art therapy can help a counselor learn what concerns a child and how the child is dealing with those concerns internally, says Judith Aron Rubin in her book, "Child Art Therapy."

Family Therapy

Family interactional patterns and dynamics offer a key to problem resolution. Through activities, children and families interact with more spontaneity and imagination than through traditional talk therapy, say Liana Lowenstein and Trudy Post Sprunk in their article, "Creative Family Therapy Techniques: Play and Art - Based Activities to Assess and Treat Families." Techniques such as family sculpting help families understand a child's perspective. Using this technique, a child creates a living sculpture by placing family members in the room in whatever position -- sitting, standing, kneeling or other position -- that best illustrates how the family members interact with each other. After discussing the sculpture, the counselor directs the child to place family members the way he would like them to be.

Talk Therapy

Talk therapy is beneficial for children who have experienced trauma, such as physical abuse, sexual abuse or the death of a loved one. Using narrative therapy, a counselor encourages a child to describe the traumatic event, and then they focus on the child's response to the event.

How to Become an Art Therapist for Children

Art therapy provides an effective and creative treatment for children with emotional, physical, mental, or social problems or disabilities. An art therapist can help children express themselves through diverse art forms and improve their functioning, confidence, and sense of well being. In order to become an art therapist for children, you'll need to get a master's degree and apply for certification before you can start looking for a job.

Part 1. Getting an Education

1. Earn your bachelor's degree. You'll need a bachelor's degree in order to enroll in an art therapy master's program. Choose psychology or studio arts as your course of study since both of these will prepare you for the types of graduate school classes you'll be taking later.

- Take courses in drawing, painting, and sculpture so that you're familiar with all of these mediums.
- Other good courses to take are human development, family studies, or developmental psychology.

2. Enroll in a master's degree program. Select an art therapy program that is approved by the American Art Therapy Association (AATA). You can visit the AATA website and search accredited programs by state. Each one will usually consist of two years of full-time education, equaling about 60 semester credits.

- If you're outside the U.S., refer to the organization in your country that gives accreditation to graduate programs to find the best one near you.
- You can also get your master's degree in counseling with an emphasis in art therapy. A counseling degree may allow you the flexibility to work in more traditional mental health fields while incorporating art therapy into your practice.

3. Focus on art therapy for children. Concentrate your studies on art therapy for children in order to prepare for your professional work later. If your program doesn't have a children's specialization, you can still focus your electives, special projects, research papers, and internship on art therapy for kids.

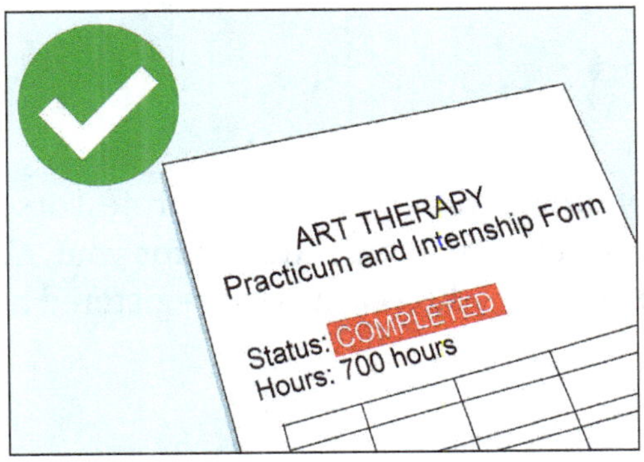

4. Complete a practicum and internship. In addition to the rest of the curriculum, you'll be required to complete at least 700 hours of supervised art therapy practice. One hundred of these hours will be part of a practicum (shadowing an art therapist) and the other 600 will be your internship (performing art therapist duties).

- Speak with professors or your academic advisor for help finding locations for your practicum and internship. They will likely know places where students have had success in the past.

Part 2. Getting Registered and Certified

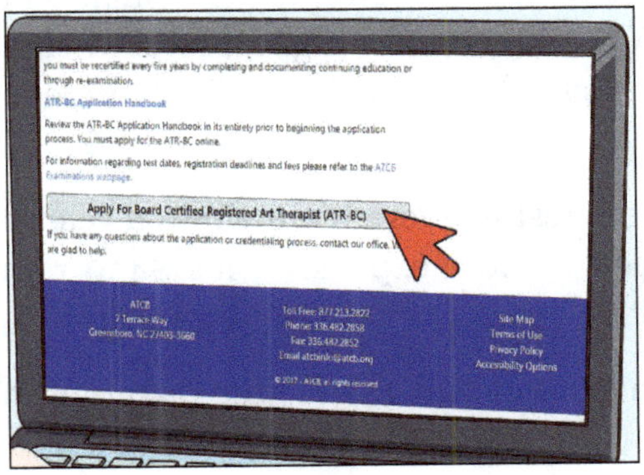

1. Apply to become a registered art therapist (ATR). Once you've earned your master's degree and

have completed your internship, you can apply to get registered through the Art Therapy Credentials Board (ATCB). Becoming an ATR will make you eligible for more job opportunities in the field.

- Visit the ATCB website for instructions on printing and submitting the application.

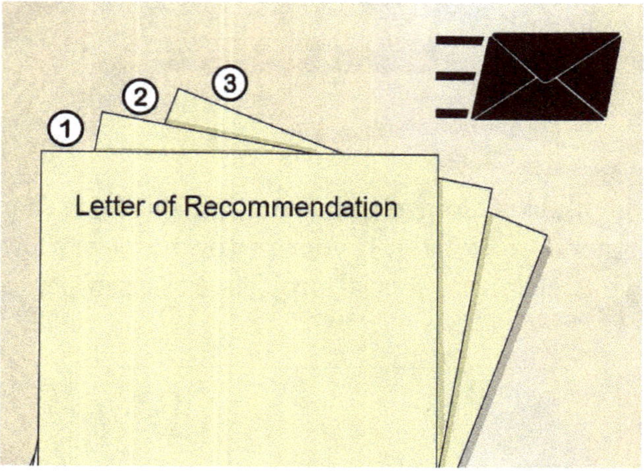

2. Submit three letters of recommendation. Ask former professors, practicum supervisors, or internship supervisors to write letters of recommendation for your ATR application. At least one of the letters should come from someone who is a current registered art therapist.

3. Take the ATR-BC examination. This is a voluntary examination that, if you pass, will show you are board certified by the ATCB and have the highest level of credentials. The paper-and-pencil test is offered once a year in November near the AATA conference site, and you must apply in September.

- The online version of the test is offered four times a year at hundreds of designated testing centers. This version is more expensive; it's $450 rather than the $260 for the paper-and-pencil test.
- Visit the ATCB website to apply and access prep materials for the test.

Part 3. Finding a Job

1. Apply where you interned. Many people seek jobs at the business or clinic where they completed their internship. Reach out to anyone you worked with to see if they have or know of any openings. Even if they don't, they'll often keep you in mind since they already know your credentials and work ethic.

2. Consult your academic network. Ask former professors and academic advisors if they know of any job openings. Some colleges provide job placement services for graduates, so visit your college's career center to see what types of services they offer.

3. Apply to jobs posted online. Search for job postings on sites like Indeed, CareerBuilder, or Linke-

dIn. Or look for more specialized job boards like PsychologyJobs.com. You can also browse the job postings page of the AATA website and filter the results by location.

4. Start your own practice. Set up a space in your home with child-sized furniture and lots of art supplies, then start seeing clients. Get the word out on social media, create a professional-looking website, and sign up to get listed on an online booking service like ZocDoc.

- If you can't use your own home, become a traveling counselor who visits clients at their homes.

How to Teach a Child Anger Management

Method 1. Teaching Coping Strategies

1. Teach The child to take deep, calming breaths when they're angry. Deep breathing can help tje child quell the physical feeling of anger in their body when it firsts rises up. Tell the child that when they feel angry, they should stop and take 10 deep breaths, in and out. Demonstrate this breathing technique and have them do it with you so they can feel its calming effect.

- This strategy will work for children of all ages as it is simple and physically calming.

2. Tell them to count backwards from 10 when they start to get upset. Engaging in a calming activity can help kids wind down when they are upset. Suggest that they try counting backwards when they first feel angry about something. This will require enough time and concentration to minimize the intensity of the child's feelings.

- Teach kids this strategy before they get mad so they can use it when their anger starts to rise. You can also remind them about it in the moment if their anger gets the best of them.

3. Encourage them to use calming self-talk when they feel like they are losing control. While getting guidance from an adult can be helpful when a child is feeling angry, they should also develop ways to reassure themselves. Tell the child to try to say calming things to themselves when they feel upset. Some simple phrases to say may include:

- "Stay cool."
- "Don't let them make you upset."
- "Try to relax."
- "Take a deep breath."
- "It's going to be okay."

4. Have the child visualize a relaxing scene to improve their mood. A positive thought can help to

improve the child's mood and relax them when they get angry. Have the child practice this kind of visualization by asking them to imagine a place where they feel calm and happy. Encourage them to think about this anytime they feel upset to ground them.

- For instance, the child may think about floating in a pool on a sunny day to make themselves feel better.
- This strategy will work better with older children who are able to focus their thoughts and feelings.

5. Suggest that they put themselves in the other person's shoes. Miscommunication and a lack of empathy can make it easy to get angry with people without hesitation. Encourage the child to think about what the other person is feeling when they are angry at someone. Emphasize that it is a very important thing to do whenever they are angry.

- For instance, if they are mad at their sister for taking their favorite toy, remind them that she watches them play with it every day and might feel jealous that she never gets to hold it.
- Younger children might have difficulty grasping this concept.

Method 2. Teaching Them to Understand Anger

1. State clearly that you understand that they are upset. Often a child's misbehaviour occurs out of a need for them to express their emotions and be heard. Help the child control these impulses

by acknowledging that you understand their frustration and anger. Knowing that someone understands what they are feeling may offer the child some comfort and relief in a difficult moment.

- For example, say something like, "I know that you are feeling angry because we couldn't go to the park today. You really wanted to play on the swings."

2. Help the child identify the warning signs that they are getting angry. To control their anger, the child needs to understand when it is building up. Talk to the child about what they feel when they are angry, and how their body feels. Help them recognize physical cues that signal that they are growing upset.

- For instance, the child might feel their heart beating faster, their fists clenching, or their cheeks getting flushed.
- Point out warning signs in the moment if you see them happening so the child can make a clear connection.

3. Have the child rate their anger on a scale of 1-10. Evaluating a child's anger can be difficult, especially if they are not able to explain why they are angry. Ask the child to give their anger a rating by assigning it a number value. This will give the child the feeling that their anger is being acknowledged, and it will help them think about how angry they really are in that moment.

- On this scale, 1 means that the child is a little angry and 10 means that the child is extremely angry.
- Having the child show you the number on their fingers will allow them to demonstrate their anger physically in a non-harmful way.

4. Notice and praise the child when they manage their anger. Encourage the child's anger management efforts by complimenting them when they demonstrate restraint. If you observe the child getting angry and then using a coping technique to calm themselves down, tell them you are proud of them. Positive reinforcement will help the child establish healthy patterns for controlling their behaviour.

- For instance, if you observe the child counting backwards from 10, say something like, "You did a great job staying calm just now."

Method 3. Addressing the Underlying Cause

1. Look for trends in the child's anger to identify an underlying issue. It is perfectly normal for a child to get angry from time to time, but a pattern of angry or out-of-control behaviour can be a warning sign of a deeper issue. Take note of the frequency and intensity of the child's angry outbursts and note any common triggers of this anger. If the child gets angry repeatedly and demonstrates the same behaviours each time, it may be because of a larger problem.

- For instance, if the child throws a tantrum every day over simple things like sitting down to eat or putting on clothes, their anger might be a cause for concern.

2. Ask them about school to see if there are any underlying problems. Sometimes the child's anger

may be due to a situation that you are unaware of, such as bullying at school or daycare. Talk to the child to see if there is anything happening that may be upsetting them. Ask them if they have had any conflicts with friends, classmates, or teachers that may be weighing on them.

- If the child won't open up to you, contact a teacher or administrator to see if there are any situations that you should be aware of.

3. Look for signs that the child may be experiencing low self-esteem. Children who experience low self-esteem may be inclined to feel frustrated and have angry outbursts. In these cases, children may benefit from speaking with a counselor or therapist to work through their feelings. Look for other signs of low self-confidence in the child, such as:

- An inclination to quit games or projects early on, often due to a fear of failure.
- Frequent mood changes, crying, or quietness.
- Self-criticism, using phrases like, "I can't do anything right" or "it's always my fault."
- Difficulty accepting both praise and criticism.
- Low grades and diminished participation in sports or other activities.
- Social withdrawal.
- Misbehaviour, such as acting disrespectfully.

4. Evaluate the child's influences to look for violent behaviour. As a general rule, children are more likely to act angrily or violently if they witness that kind of behaviour on a regular basis. Look at the child's day-to-day influences to see if there are any demonstrations of aggression or negativity that may be affecting them. These influences may include their friends, relatives, favorite television shows, video games, or comic books.

- Exposure to violence in television shows or movies can make kids less sensitive to it, making it easier to be physically aggressive without worrying about the consequences.
- If you suspect that the behaviour of a family friend or relative is negatively influencing the child, talk to them about controlling their behaviour.

5. Seek professional help if you suspect the child may have a mental health disorder. In some cases, guidance from a child therapist or counselor may be the best approach to helping your child with their anger. If the child shows a persistent pattern of angry outbursts and aggression, ask their pediatrician for a referral to a mental health professional with ample experience with children. the child's anger may be due to an underlying mental disorder such as:

- ADHA
- Anxiety
- Autism
- An undiagnosed learning disorder

Method 4. Setting a Good Example

1. Be mindful of how you interact with other people around the child. the child will observe your behaviour at all times, not just when you are addressing them directly. Make sure to be calm and respectful in all of your interactions with other people so that you child doesn't see you lose your cool. If you are rude to others or yell at someone around the child, you will not be able to reprimand them when they show the same behaviour.

- For instance, if a waiter at a restaurant makes a mistake with your order, be calm and understanding about it instead of berating them.

2. Step away from arguments with the child to avoid getting angry. If the child is throwing a temper tantrum or acting aggressively towards you, it can be difficult to remain calm. If you are unable to keep your composure, take a "time out" and go into another room for a few minutes. Exit calmly and come back once you feel that you can deal with the child's anger in a healthy way.

- Before leaving, say something like, "I need to take a 'time out' to control my emotions" so that the child knows why you are stepping away.
- Doing this will also help the child understand that "time outs" are not just a punishment for them, but an opportunity to calm down and gain control.

3. Tell the child that you forgive them for misbehaving. Give the child a positive example of compassion by forgiving them after they get angry with you. Acknowledge that they behaved badly but let them know that it doesn't make them a bad person. Feeling the relief of your forgiveness may encourage them to show the same compassion to people themselves.

- For example, say, "It wasn't nice of you to scream at me earlier, but I know you were angry and didn't mean to upset me. I forgive you.

How to Help a Depressed Child

Method 1. Seeking Professional Help and Treatment

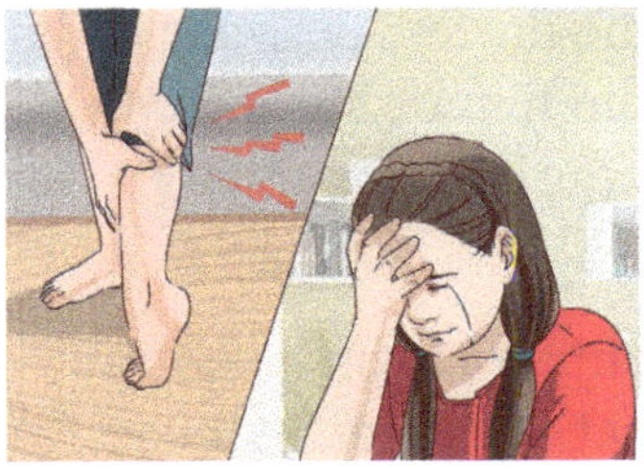

1. Recognizing the signs of depression in a child. Depression comes with a host of typical signs

in any person. These symptoms can often manifest themselves differently in children. Noticing if your child has any signs of depression can help you more readily identify a potential problem and seek professional help in a timely manner. Your child may be depressed if he or she has the following signs:

- Being sad, irritable, tearful, or cranky most of the day
- Showing an inability to enjoy the things that he or she used to
- Showing significant changes in weight, either up or down
- Sleeping too little at night or too much during the day
- Wanting to be alone
- Lacking energy or feeling an inability to do even simple tasks
- Feeling worthless or guilty
- Having trouble concentrating or making choices
- Having little or no care about the future
- Having aches or pains when nothing is wrong
- Thinking frequently about death or suicide

2. Schedule an appointment with a doctor. Depression is not something you can treat on your own. The best way to help your child is to get professional treatment. Call your child's doctor and make an appointment. Let the office know what it's for so that the staff can get your child in as soon as possible. Depression can be treated in more than 80% of the people who have it.

- Tell your child that you're concerned about the way he or she has been feeling and that you're taking him or her to the doctor. Let your child know that depression is normal and that seeing the doctor can help him or her feel much better. Make sure you tell your child to be honest when talking to the doctor so that he or she can get the best help available to overcome depression.
- Let the doctor know any symptoms you've noticed in your child and ask any questions you may have. Remember that when you're answering questions to also give your child a chance to speak.

3. Get a referral to a mental health professional. Your child's doctor may refer him or her to a mental health professional. These individuals can help your child manage his or her depression, especially if your child feels comfortable with the person. If a person is not a good fit with your child, try another professional. Ask your doctor which of the following mental health professionals might be right to help your child:

- Psychiatrist, which is a medical doctor who can diagnose and treat depression as well as prescribe medicine.
- Psychologist, which is a health professional who can diagnose and treat depression but may not write prescriptions.
- Licensed clinical social worker, which is an individual who has a degree in social work and is qualified to treat your child's depression.

4. Take anti-depressant medications. Treatment for depression in children is often a combination of psychotherapy and medication. Giving your child prescribed anti-depressants can help relieve the symptoms of his or depression.

- Be aware that the Food and Drug Administration has only approved two drugs for use in children. These are fluoxetine (Prozac) and escitalopram (Lexapro). Prozac is approved for children over the age of eight and Lexapro for children over 12. These medications may increase the risk of suicidal thinking or behavior in children and you should closely monitor your child if he or she is taking an anti-depressant.
- Keep in mind that it can take two to four weeks for antidepressants to begin working for your child. Use therapy and self-care to help your child during this period. Many doctors may have your child gradually stop taking the medication after six to 12 months.

- Make sure your child takes his or her medications as directed every day. This is one of the biggest ways you can help him or her with depression.
- Talk to your doctor or psychiatrist if your child is under 8 and suffering from depression.

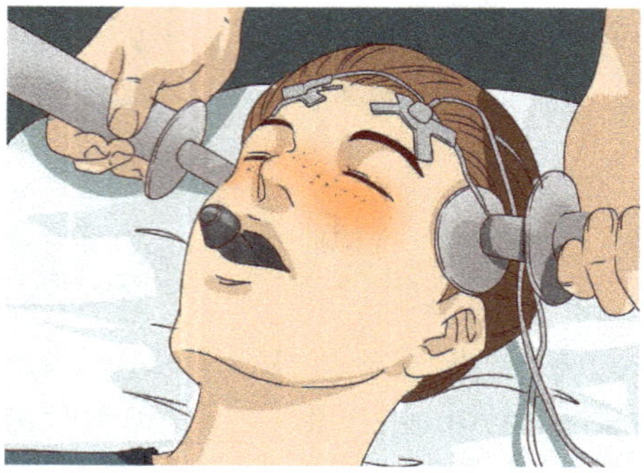

5. Consider alternative treatments. Your child's doctor may want to try alternative treatments if therapy, medication, and self-care are not working. From hospital stays to electroconvulsive therapy, these alternative treatments may help relieve your child's depression. Some of the alternative treatments you may want to think about for your child are:

- A hospital stay or outpatient day treatment for your child if he or she is really struggling with depression.
- Electroconvulsive therapy, or ECT, is a surgical procedure in which electrical currents are passed to the brain to improve brain function. Despite many misperceptions, it is safe for children and often has a high response rate, which means it can help a child with depression relatively quickly.
- Transcranial magnetic stimulation, or TMS, which can help those children who don't respond to anti-depressants. For this procedure, a treatment coil is placed against the scalp to send a magnetic pulse that stimulates nerve cells involved in mood regulation. Although doctors are still gathering evidence on the efficacy of TMS in children, it is safe and may help your child if other treatments aren't working.

Method 2. Helping a Depressed Child at Work

1. Stay informed of local and laws and organizational policies. If you're a teacher or childcare worker, it's natural to want to help a child who is struggling with depression. However, how you can help may be governed by federal and local laws as well as organizational policies. Keeping yourself

abreast of any laws and protocols related to providing depressed children with help can ensure that you assist the child in a way that doesn't violate his or her rights. It also minimizes the risk of a lawsuit for you or the organization.

- Ask your school principal or other legal administrator what you are able to do. Make sure to inform the principal, school nurse, or counselor if you're trying to help a depressed child. They may be unaware that the child is depressed and need to file for something such as an Individualized Educational Plan.
- Avoid telling anyone other than someone in authority about your suspicions or knowledge of the child's depression. Keep in mind that depression is a medical condition and falls under medical privacy laws in most countries.

2. Let the child know you are willing to help. Even just telling a child who is depressed that you will help him or her can give comfort to get through the day. As far as you are able, tell the child that you are open to talk or will give him or her consideration when it comes to work, chores, or other activities and tasks.

- Assure the child that there is no pressure to talk or ask for help. Just let him or her know that your door is always open to listen to problems and give help where you can. For example, say, "I know you're struggling, Sara. You can come to me and talk any time you like. I'm also handy at helping with homework if you need that or a quiet space to work."
- Offer to allow the student to stop by and help you with something during the day. This gives him or her the opportunity to address any problems in a safe environment but also gives you a chance to bolster the child's confidence with some positive feedback.

3. Stay patient and understanding. A depressed child may feel like the world is working against

him or her and any little sign of impatience from another person may aggravate the depression. Reminding yourself that the child is depressed and needs a bit of a break can help you remain patient and understanding if he or she slips up occasionally.

- Take a deep breath if you feel like you're going to scold the child. This can help relax you and the situation.

4. Provide constructive criticism along with two positive comments. When a child is depressed, he or she may focus on negative comments rather than on anything positive. That is why it is important to avoid making negative comments and to deliver constructive criticism in a positive way. If you have constructive criticism for this child, then make sure that you "sandwich" it between two positive comments.

- For example, "Riley, you've done such a great job with these problems. Do you think you could try one or two more? That would give you the chance to show the other kids your knowledge."

5. Provide regular breaks. Depressed children can become easily overwhelmed and anxious in situations such as school or intramural activities. Giving the child regular breaks to rest and relax can help calm him or her and boost confidence.

- Allow the child to put his or her head on a desk in the back of the room. You can also let the child leave the classroom and go to the nurse if he or she asks. If you have assemblies, fire drills, or other activities that may make the depression worse, give the child a chance to take a break from them or go somewhere else.

- Give the child a colored card or something else to indicate he or she needs a break without drawing attention to him or herself. The child can put it on his or her desk, or even on yours.

6. Accommodate tasks to the child's specific needs. Some children with depression will have Individualized Education Programs, but others may not. Make sure to follow the IEP if you have it—these are specifically tailored to the child's condition. If the child doesn't have an IEP, make appropriate accommodation to help the child. This can be a broad range of things such as:

- Seating the child in a place he or she is comfortable.
- Calling on the child only when it's a topic with which he or she is confident.
- Giving the child an alternative location in which to take tests.
- Giving them alternative homework and testing assignments.
- Offering extra support when the child has missed school.

Child Abuse Counseling

Child abuse counseling is a special field of counseling that focuses on treating children that have suffered at the hands of a trusted loved one. Patients of child abuse psychologists might be victims of abuse themselves, or they might have witnessed a loved one being abused, such as a parent or sibling.

As a career, child abuse counseling can be as difficult as they come. Professionals will often witness the marks and scars on children - visible or otherwise - on children each and every day of their professional lives. They might recognize signs of a few different common types of child abuse. Here are a few examples of the atrocities that child abuse counselors may bear witness to:

- Physical Abuse - Intentionally aggressive actions on a child that inflict pain.
- Emotional & Psychological Abuse - Cruel behavior that cause mental anguish or damage to one's mental state.
- Neglect - The absence of parental care. Lack of supervision, proper diet, medical attention, shelter, and safe conditions.

- Sexual Abuse - Any type of behavior that is sexual in nature, or intended to provide the offender with sexual stimulation.

There was once a time that child abuse, as we define it today, was not talked about. In the case of physical abuse, for instance, a parent striking a child was not uncommon and even expected at certain times. In 1875, however, this attitude began to change, when Mary Ellen Wilson, an eight year old little girl was found to have been badly abused by her step-mother. Etta Angell Wheeler, a missionary and social worker, was asked by a neighbor to investigate the case. Upon finding evidence of abuse and neglect, Wheeler turned to the local American Society for the Prevention of Cruelty to Animals, because there were no laws restricting child abuse at that time. Eventually, Mary Ellen Wilson was removed from her home and adopted by Wheeler and her family.

This case was one of the most shocking of its time, and it ultimately led to the creation of the New York Society for the Prevention of Cruelty to Children.

Today, we now have laws against all types of child abuse. However, it still remains a big problem, in the United States and across the globe. Child abuse counselors are the compassionate professionals that dedicate their live to trying to reverse the effects of abuse, one little life at a time.

Child Abuse Counselor

Child abuse counselors typically work closely with child victims of abuse. They are often called upon to help recognize possible signs of abuse in a child. Listed below are several indicators of child abuse:

- Physical Abuse - Unexplained bruises, cuts, or other injuries. Child flinches when touched.
- Emotional Abuse - Withdrawn or overly shy, excessively low self-esteem. Extreme behavior.
- Sexual Abuse - Inappropriate touching or fondling of other children. Trouble sitting or walking
- Neglect - Poor hygiene. Clothes ill fitting, dirty, or inappropriate

Once a child abuse counselor has an idea of the type of abuse a child has suffered, she will then attempt to get the child to open up about his experience. This is often a difficult task, since abuse is traumatizing to many children, and it can make them leery to trust any adults. Before this next step can be achieved, a child abuse counselor must be able to earn the trust of the abused child. This often takes copious amounts of compassion and patience. A child must usually feel comfortable in the presence of a child abuse counselor.

There are a few ways that a counselor can get an abused child to open up about his experience. First of all, she must be friendly, approachable, and non-judgmental. Many child abuse counselors will also use a concept known as play therapy. This process involves encouraging children to play, which can lead to them opening up about their experiences. A child may be asked to play with a doll, for instance, or draw pictures. More often than not, a child will reveal his experiences while "playing". For example, a victim of sexual abuse might touch a doll inappropriately, much as his abuser touched him.

Once a child abuse counselor knows more about the type and severity of the abuse, she can then begin treatment. While recovering from abuse, one of the most important things that a child abuse counselor can communicate to her patient is that the abuse was not his fault. She may also need to treat any psychological and emotional problems caused by the abuse, such as depression, anxiety, or post-traumatic stress syndrome.

A child abuse counselor will also usually work with caregivers, like parents, foster parents, or other legal guardians. She may instruct them on how to act around the child and what to expect during the recovery process.

How to Become a Child Abuse Counselor

In order to be licensed as a child abuse counselor, it is required that an individual obtain at least a Master's degree. Some pursue a doctoral degree to further their education and attain the highest professional clout they can. Many candidates pursue Master's degrees in counseling or related fields such as social work, marriage and family therapy, or counseling psychology, where the median salary in 2015 was between $41,880 and $45,900 according to The Bureau of Labor Statistics. It takes quite a bit of education to become a licensed counselor, but a person can begin exploring the field by volunteering at a crisis shelter.

Child Abuse Counselor Certification and Education

Education for Child Abuse Counselors will provide you the necessary requirements to be able to work effectively and safely as a professional counselor. Working with children in the role of child abuse counselor is one of the most sensitive and important careers possible. Those looking to become child abuse counselors are required to be credentialed mental health counselors who have work experience in different forms of abuse. Child abuse counselors are highly trained and work with young and old victims of childhood abuse. In some instances, the counselor will only work with abusers. They type of therapy these counselors use will be based on the client.

In most cases, children have a positive reaction to therapy that involves play. Nowadays, parents will see out a counselor who uses the practice. Counselors may choose to prescribe therapy that ranges from play therapy to one-on-one conversation. Sometimes the counselor may choose to use cognitive therapy. Each therapy's purpose is to help the child understand that they didn't do anything to deserve abuse. Counselors provide the child with a space to talk about the abuse and the words to explain themselves.

Find schools and get information on the program that's right for you.

Find Programs

During therapy, the counselor will asses the child's progress through goals that they have set based on how old the child is and their level of development. Counselors may be part of a unified team that includes key social workers, nurses, and doctors. Often, the family of the client is supportive and wants to be involved in the therapy process. In cases like this, therapy will be conducted while involving the family members and children.

Children that have found themselves victims of childhood abuse often times suffer from PTSD, anxiety or other nervous disorders. In therapy, children are taught how to reduce their stress and relax. Some counselors will seek out treatment centers that specialize in these types of therapies.

Licensing and Certification

Typically, states are going to require child abuse counselors, like other counselors, to be credentialed according to the standards set by that states board. Prior to obtaining full credentials as a counselor, the candidate will need to successfully complete an examination and overseen practice hours. Background checks are required by all looking to become counselors. Child abuse counselors in some situations may be allowed to achieve lower level credentials while accumulating hours, they may also receive certifications in fields such as play therapy.

The Need for Counseling All Survivors of Abuse

Many survivors of abuse are now adults; this represents another major segment of the population that needs treatment. Traditionally, sexual abuse was underreported; unfortunately, the perceived stigma of reporting kept many people from doing so. Therefore, many victims have not received the treatment they need. Very often, adult survivors may have developed a variety of mental health issues as a result of the past abuse. Often, there is the manifestation of anxiety and other neuroses. Depending on the person, they may be too protective of their child and others might be too distant. In some people they might not know what the right amount of affection is or find affection off-putting. Counselors are needed to help patients discover connections, or correlations, between their current issues and abuse sustained in the past.

How to Guide your Clients on Handling Child after Child Abuse

Building Resilience and Promoting Protective Factors

Resilience is a child or youth's ability to cope, and even thrive, following a negative experience. This is not an inherent trait but something that has to be developed and nurtured.

Some of the ways you can help your child build resilience include:

- Build strong connections with friends and family that can support children during challenges and teach them to think about and consider other people's feelings.

- Allow children to feel their feelings. Teach them how to describe those feelings, and commend them for expressing feelings of hurt or sadness without acting out.
- Be consistent. If you say you'll be there, be there. If you say you'll listen to concerns, listen. This will help to teach your child that people can be trusted.
- Be patient. Children's reactions to trauma vary as widely as the types of trauma one can experience. There isn't a one-size-fits-all solution.
- Express your support. Express love and support for your child verbally and physically. Express your love through words, notes, and hugs.
- Teach your child the importance of healthy behaviors. Have open and honest talks about the dangers of drugs and alcohol, smoking, and sexual promiscuity. Teach your child the importance of eating properly and exercising.

Experiencing abuse or neglect doesn't mean your child will develop poor health or negative well-being outcomes. When caregivers and parents foster protective factors—circumstances in families and communities that increase the health and well-being of children and families—it may lessen the negative effects of maltreatment. A strong and secure emotional bond between children and their caregivers is critical for children's physical, social, and emotional development, including their ability to form trusting relationships, exhibit positive behaviors, and heal from past traumas.

The healing process is not always a clear, straight path, and it takes time. Some things you can do to help your child heal include:

- Address the child's physical safety first by letting him or her know that no one will physically lash out. This will help the child create feelings of trust and open up to psychological and emotional healing.
- Address the past as the past. Help the child identify elements of his or her current life that are different from the past. Use this as an opportunity to discuss new boundaries and expectations to encourage feelings of belonging and attachment.

Building a Strong Relationship With Your Child

A child's earliest relationships are some of the most important. Attachment is the sense of security and safety a child feels with caregivers and is important for your child's physical, emotional, mental, and psychological development. It is formed through consistent, positive affection and emotional interactions. The issues and challenges most caregivers face with children who have experienced maltreatment is the result of a break in attachment during the first 3 years of life.

To foster a secure relationship with a child:

- Be available. Provide consistent support to build feelings of trust and safety.
- Offer comfort. Support the child when he or she is upset, modeling appropriate displays of affection and building the child's self-esteem.
- Be respectful. Let your child know that you will keep him or her safe.

Difference Between Child Abuse and Child Discipline

It is normal for children to act out and challenge a parent or caregiver's authority. Toddlers throw tantrums. Teenagers argue. The ways in which parents guide a child and discipline poor behavior is critical to shaping more positive behavior. Children learn control and self-discipline from their caregivers, and discipline should never be harmful to a child. In fact, severe punishment won't accomplish your goals and can do more harm than good. For children who have experienced abuse or neglect, aggressive punishment could elicit memories of past trauma or cause retraumatization.

Discipline and punishment, while often used interchangeably, are actually quite different.

- Discipline is the act of teaching children the difference between acceptable and unacceptable behavior. This can be accomplished by talking to children about misbehavior and requiring children to take responsibility for its consequences, like being responsible for cleaning up a mess or apologizing for hurting someone's feelings. You also can guide your child by positively reinforcing and encouraging their good behaviors and not just correcting their poor behaviors.
- Punishment is an approach to discipline that can be physical—a slap on the hand—or psychological—the loss of TV time, or other freedoms. (Center for Early Education and Development, n.d.).

A misbehaving child can be frustrating, but using physical force to teach a lesson or relieve aggravation is always wrong. Factors like sleep and diet can cause tensions to rise. If your child is acting out and you feel overwhelmed, consider whether he or she is hungry, tired, or expressing a reaction to an underlying issue like fear or anxiety.

Practical Discipline Tips or Techniques

The following tips may help you safely discipline your child:

- Role modeling: Children learn more about behavior by watching adults than in any other way. Be a positive example for expressing emotions and dealing with frustration. Stay calm instead of yelling.
- Encouragement: Let children know what they are doing right as well as pointing out the mistakes they make.
- Rules: Set routines for bedtimes, meals, and chores. Knowing what will happen next can be very important to a child whose life once felt chaotic.
- Set limits: Be very clear about your limits.
- Attention-ignore: Ignoring behavior is simply pretending that the behavior is not occurring. The parent does not look at, talk to, or respond to the child until the inappropriate behavior ends. When a child breaks a rule, stay calm and do what is fair. Sometimes, your child can help you decide what is fair to do when a rule is broken.
- Never hit or shake a child: Hitting is not a useful discipline tool for your children. Besides the potential physical abuse and injury, hitting and other physical punishments are not

effective ways to discipline. They teach children that it is acceptable to hurt people, and they make children much too angry to be sorry for what they've done.

- Gear the discipline to the child's developmental stage: Don't expect a child of any age to perform something he or she is not ready for. Allow your child to learn at his or her own pace. Break tasks down into small, manageable steps, so that he or she feels a sense of success and accomplishment.

Permissions

All chapters in this book are published with permission under the Creative Commons Attribution Share Alike License or equivalent. Every chapter published in this book has been scrutinized by our experts. Their significance has been extensively debated. The topics covered herein carry significant information for a comprehensive understanding. They may even be implemented as practical applications or may be referred to as a beginning point for further studies.

We would like to thank the editorial team for lending their expertise to make the book truly unique. They have played a crucial role in the development of this book. Without their invaluable contributions this book wouldn't have been possible. They have made vital efforts to compile up to date information on the varied aspects of this subject to make this book a valuable addition to the collection of many professionals and students.

This book was conceptualized with the vision of imparting up-to-date and integrated information in this field. To ensure the same, a matchless editorial board was set up. Every individual on the board went through rigorous rounds of assessment to prove their worth. After which they invested a large part of their time researching and compiling the most relevant data for our readers.

The editorial board has been involved in producing this book since its inception. They have spent rigorous hours researching and exploring the diverse topics which have resulted in the successful publishing of this book. They have passed on their knowledge of decades through this book. To expedite this challenging task, the publisher supported the team at every step. A small team of assistant editors was also appointed to further simplify the editing procedure and attain best results for the readers.

Apart from the editorial board, the designing team has also invested a significant amount of their time in understanding the subject and creating the most relevant covers. They scrutinized every image to scout for the most suitable representation of the subject and create an appropriate cover for the book.

The publishing team has been an ardent support to the editorial, designing and production team. Their endless efforts to recruit the best for this project, has resulted in the accomplishment of this book. They are a veteran in the field of academics and their pool of knowledge is as vast as their experience in printing. Their expertise and guidance has proved useful at every step. Their uncompromising quality standards have made this book an exceptional effort. Their encouragement from time to time has been an inspiration for everyone.

The publisher and the editorial board hope that this book will prove to be a valuable piece of knowledge for students, practitioners and scholars across the globe.

Index

Printed in the USA
CPSIA information can be obtained
at www.ICGtesting.com
LVHW080031211023
761596LV00010BA/1719

9 781639 898107